Teddy Bears

A Collectible History
of the Teddy Bear

Kathy Martin

Bath New York Singapore Hong Kong Cologne Delhi Melbourne

First published in 2007
Parragon
Queen Street House
4 Queen Street
Bath BA1 1HE, UK

ISBN 978-1-4054-8667-5

Produced by Butler and Tanner
Project Editor: Julian Flanders
Editor: Helen Burge
Designer: Carole McDonald

Printed in China

CONTENTS

INTRODUCTION

The teddy bear is something of a paradox. Many people are attracted to its comforting appearance – an instant reminder of a safe and idyllic childhood, whether real or imaginary. But that familiar bear is in many ways an illusion; for the century or so that the teddy bear has been with us it's had more facelifts and makeovers than any Hollywood film star. What makes it so remarkable is that for all the endless reinventing, the basic concept of the stuffed, five-way jointed toy bear has stayed pretty much the same. The impossible trick the teddy bear has pulled off is to adopt any number of new guises whilst retaining its identity as the toy we know and love. In doing so, it has extended its appeal far beyond the safe confines of the Edwardian nursery into the noisy, hectic and sometimes downright alarming reality of the 21st century.

Today the teddy bear remains as popular as it has ever been. Traditionally associated with childhood comfort and safety, it has somehow made the leap from much-loved toy to universal icon of emotional security. For many of today's technologically-aware youngsters, computer games are all very well but when it comes to the crunch, nothing beats cuddling a teddy. It's not just children who love teddy bears, though. The truth is that most adults have a soft spot for them, and a surprising number are truly passionate about them, amassing large collections of teddy bears and everything connected with them. Known as 'arctophiles', a word derived by combining the Greek words for bear – *arctos* and lover – *philos*, these enthusiasts come from all generations and all walks of life. They can be anything from bankers to builders, housewives to hoteliers – people linked only by their love of the teddy bear.

Psychologists and authors have spent much time trying to analyze why so many of us find it impossible to resist the teddy bear's appeal. One theory suggests we are responding to a nostalgic impulse to recapture our lost childhood and that seems like a reasonable suggestion. Whatever the deeper psychological reasons for our abiding love affair with the teddy bear may be, we must acknowledge a debt of gratitude to the man who invented it. This book examines how the teddy bear has retained his place as the world's favorite toy throughout the last 100 years by constantly reinventing himself, but it is impossible to do this without first taking a brief look at how he came into existence in the first place.

THE FIRST TEDDY BEAR

The 'father of the teddy bear' is generally held to be Richard Steiff, nephew of an inspirational German woman called Margarete Steiff. Despite the fact that polio left her confined to a wheelchair from infancy, Margarete went on to found a soft toy factory that became world famous for its high quality products. Her story is remarkable and moving, but the honor of creating the world's favorite toy fell to her talented nephew, Richard, in 1902.

Before Richard Steiff's jointed bear came along, toy bears did exist but they were completely unlike what we now know as the teddy bear. Real bears featured heavily in European folk tales, and they were frequently used to scare naughty children into behaving well. Many terrified youngsters must have gone to bed with the threat that 'the bears will get you if you disobey' ringing in their ears. This impression of the bear as a scary and vicious character was reinforced by the miserable dancing bears that were routinely used to entertain folk in Europe and North America. Half-starved and beaten, these bears stood on their hind legs as they performed their dreary routines, often with a heavy chain or rope around their necks. Consequently, when the bear was produced in toy form, it

appeared in a similar pose, sometimes baring its teeth in a snarl. Whether crudely carved from wood and sold as a cheap fairground memento, or lovingly crafted as a clockwork automation and sold at the luxury end of the market, the result was the same – a faintly sinister toy as unlike the warm and comforting teddy we know today as it is possible to imagine.

A man ahead of his time in many ways, Richard Steiff sought to redress the balance in the bear's favor by creating a toy bear that would win children's hearts. As the 19th century drew to a close, he spent time sketching bears wherever possible, and experimented with various methods of creating the huggable bear of his imagination. Early attempts, whilst charming in their own right, were not entirely satisfactory but then, in 1902, he hit upon the idea of using string joints to make a bear that had movement. The new design was called Bär PB55 – the P referring to the fact that he was made of plush, the B standing for *Beweglich*, the German word for movable, and the 55 referring to his size in centimetres when seated. Today we know PB55 as the world's first teddy bear, but it was to be another six years before Steiff started using the term as a name for their soft, jointed bears, and before then many changes had been made to the original design. History records that Margarete Steiff was unconvinced by her nephew's new toy, but Richard knew he was close to achieving his aim and he continued to experiment, producing subsequent bears which were first thread (Bär PB35) and then rod-jointed (Bär PB28). Finally, in 1905 he unveiled Bär PAB35, a disc-jointed bear that met his own high standards and of which his aunt thoroughly approved, so much so that she

LEFT: Margarete Steiff, founder of the world famous Steiff company.

OPPOSITE (left): A mint condition apricot-colored Steiff, circa 1905, sold at Christie's in 2000 for $9,160.
(middle): Edwina, a beautiful white Steiff teddy bear from the late 1920s; she has been well cared for and therefore remains in excellent condition.
(right): An original gray Richard Steiff bear.

LEFT: Richard Steiff, Margarete's nephew, admiring his perfected bear.
MIDDLE: A modern Steiff replica of PB55, their very first jointed bear – sadly none are known to have survived to this day.
RIGHT: PB25 and PB35, early incarnations of the Steiff teddy bear.

dubbed the new design *Bärle*, a German term of endearment. She wasn't the only one to love Richard's perfected bear – by 1906 400,000 had been sold, and Steiff had a significant hit on their hands.

AMERICAN GODFATHERS

Although the first jointed bear was created in Germany, it was in America that he got his name and shot to fame. In fact, if Richard Steiff can be called the father of the teddy bear, then two prominent Americans – Theodore Roosevelt, President of the United States, and Clifford K. Berryman, a cartoonist for the *Washington Post* – should be called its godfathers. In November 1902, the same year that Bär PB55 was getting a lukewarm reception from Margarete Steiff, Roosevelt, known affectionately as 'Teddy' to his friends, set off on a trip to negotiate in a border dispute between the States of Louisiana and Mississippi. As the President was a keen sportsman, his hosts thoughtfully arranged for him to go on a bear hunt during his stay, but the bears in the vicinity had other ideas and made themselves scarce. With no bears to shoot the trip was a disaster. Some desperate member of the President's entourage sought to rectify things by catching an old and infirm bear and tying

it to a tree, gift-wrapped, as it were, for the President. These sort of shenanigans were beneath Roosevelt, however, and shooting a captive bear was not his idea of sport. He declined to shoot it, although the bear was killed in any case, by knife instead of by gun.

Perhaps it was a slow news week because the story of the President's refusal to shoot the bear made the headlines. Clifford K. Berryman sketched the incident for his paper and captioned it 'Drawing the Line in Mississippi', an allusion to the boundary dispute that had brought Roosevelt to the area as well as to his decision not to shoot the bear. From the moment that the Berryman cartoon hit the newsstands, Roosevelt was instantly associated with the bear, and almost within days his nickname, Teddy, was being used for the new jointed toy bears that were appearing in the shops. Roosevelt went on to fight and win the 1904 presidential election with the teddy bear as his mascot, and highly collectable memorabilia from this time can still be found today. As an adjunct to this story, a few years ago I interviewed Tweed Roosevelt, a great-nephew of Theodore, and he told me that at one point the President had considered adopting the bull moose as his official mascot instead of the bear. Had he done so, it is debatable

plush, or art silk, was introduced to the teddy bear industry, although mohair remained the first choice for quality teddy bears right up to the 1950s when nylon and other man-made materials became widespread. During the Second World War, with kapok in short supply, a by-product of the cotton industry known as 'sub' was used to stuff bears, and from the 1950s onwards foam was introduced.

Following Steiff and Ideal's lead, more American and German companies began producing the fashionable new toy, many of them preferring to copy Steiff's designs rather than go to the trouble of creating their own. Steiff's famous button in ear trademark, introduced in 1904, gave customers a valuable assurance of quality but didn't prevent their ideas being copied. Two of their early German rivals, Gebruder Bing and Strunz, were so persistent in their copying that Steiff had to take legal action. With a background in mechanical toys, Bing soon found their niche producing wonderful clockwork bears that are highly prized by

whether the jointed bear would have achieved the iconic status it has today.

The final characters in the story of the early days of the teddy bear were a Russian émigré called Morris Michtom and his wife, Rose. They were inspired by Berryman's cartoon to make a toy bear which they put in the window of their Brooklyn novelty store, with a little sign describing it as Teddy's Bear. The bear sold, so Rose made some more and they were also snapped up speedily. Sadly, no picture exists to show us what these bears looked like – a great pity because it would be fascinating to see how they compared with Steiff's jointed bear. In the absence of the evidence, we have to assume that they were very appealing because demand outstripped the Michtoms' ability to produce them. Luckily, a local company stepped in to help, and thus the Ideal Novelty and Toy Co. – the first American teddy bear manufacturer – was born.

Early teddy bears were made of mohair and stuffed with fine wood shavings known as wood-wool or excelsior. Their eyes were the small round buttons used to fasten shoes and boots. Boot buttons gave way to glass eyes, and in the 1920s wood-wool was replaced by a softer natural stuffing called kapok. In 1929, a man-made material called artificial silk

'Drawing the line in Mississippi' – the Clifford K. Berryman cartoon that led to the new jointed toy bear being dubbed 'Teddy's bear'.

TOP LEFT: This 1906 image of Steiff bears enjoying a hug was used for a 'Friends for life' advertising campaign.

collectors today. Sadly, the company went out of business in 1932. Strunz was even shorter lived – they are not believed to have survived beyond the First World War. Steiff, on the other hand, continued to flourish, thanks to a combination of consistently brilliant design, clever marketing and careful quality control. In 1907 they made nearly a million teddy bears, and although that record has yet to be broken, they remain in the ascendancy today, having outlasted by decades most of their early competitors.

For every company that floundered, however, a dozen others sprang up to take its place. Today, as well as Steiff, the names of just a handful of German firms – Cramer, Hermann, Schreyer & Co (Schuco), Josef Pitrmann (JoPi) and Petz amongst them – are familiar to collectors, and their bears sell well at auction. Their success is partly due to the quality of the bears but it also has something to do with the relative longevity of the firms – they were around long enough for people to remember them. Many perfectly good German-made bears of yesteryear can sell for low prices simply because their manufacturers didn't stay the course and their names have fallen into obscurity.

It is a similar story with the American teddy pioneers. As demand for the teddy bear grew, entrepreneurial people took to manufacturing them with gusto but just a fraction of the firms are remembered today. Ideal led the way, and the Bruin Manufacturing Company is known to have been making teddy bears as early as 1907, as was the Aetna Toy Animal Company. Hecla worked hard to imitate Steiff's bears but success was elusive and they didn't last long. A company that showed great staying power, on the other hand, was Gund, which had been making soft toys including stuffed bears since 1899. Their first actual teddy bear is thought to date from 1906, and to them goes the accolade of being the USA's oldest existing teddy bear manufacturer. The Knickerbocker Toy Company added teddy bears and other cuddly animals to its range of toys in the 1920s, and became a key player in the history of the American teddy, notably producing Smokey Bear under licence in the 1970s. The firm went out of business in the 1980s, around the same time that Ideal was sold to another toy manufacturer and bears were dropped from production. There is some comfort in the fact that the company had survived long enough to celebrate its 75th anniversary in 1978, and a special bear was produced to mark the occasion.

The teddy craze reached Britain in 1908 and some existing toy manufacturers produced their own examples around this time, the first of these probably being J.K. Farnell. By and large, though, customers were happy to buy German bears until the outbreak of the First World War put an end to that, and almost overnight a flourishing British teddy bear industry was born.

During the First World War, Farnell produced miniature jointed bears which were given as good luck mementoes to soldiers setting off for the Front. Made in a choice of golden, red, white or blue mohair, these little bears are sometimes found at auction today, evocative survivors of a desperate conflict. Harwin & Co was another firm that marketed bears with a military angle. Founded in 1914, they are famous for their patriotic Ally Bears which were dressed in the uniforms of various regiments, but they ceased all production in 1930. That same year, coincidentally, a company called Merrythought was launched in historic Ironbridge, Shropshire, England, employing two senior managers from

Farnell and Chad Valley, another leading soft toy manufacturer, to steer their path towards success in the industry. The company is still producing quality teddy bears today, and is justifiably proud of the fact that they are hand made in England. They also gave the world the Cheeky Bear, one of the most popular and idiosyncratic of all teddy bears.

As with the German and American manufacturers, British firms came and went, but the ones that are best remembered today are Farnell, Dean's, Chad Valley, Merrythought and Chiltern. As far as collectors of British teddy bears are concerned, early Farnells are the holy grail but they are correspondingly expensive, while everyone loves – and most can afford – a Chiltern's Hugmee. One of the most noteworthy firms from the post-Second World War era was Wendy Boston Playsafe Toys, which invented lock-in safety eyes in 1948, and fully washable, nylon bears

in 1954. Having enjoyed enormous commercial success for a decade or so, the company was bought by a larger toy manufacturer in 1968, and ceased production in 1976.

Since those early days the teddy has conquered the world with his gentle, unassuming ways. Few nations have not at one time or another boasted their own teddy manufacturer, and the genre of teddy bear literature is huge in many countries. Teddy Bears have starred on TV, radio and film, they have inspired hit records, been the subject of comic strips and ad campaigns, and have been the mascots of multi-million dollar fundraising initiatives. Down the decades, through good times and bad, the teddy bear has retained his place in our hearts, and he's done it by never being predictable. You never know what his next incarnation is going to be, which is why clever Teddy is such a master of disguise.

CLOCKWISE (from left): A group of beautiful, early Steiff teddy bears; Miles, a blond Steiff teddy bear dating from 1908, whose worn appearance rather adds to his charm: Pooh, an English teddy of unknown origin, *circa* 1920; Berryman Bear, created by the Ideal Novelty and Toy Company, *circa* 1904.

OPPOSITE: Sebastian, a lovely brown Steiff, *circa* 1920.

Some teddy bear designs have proved enduringly popular over the years, maintaining their market share as other models blazed briefly and then faded from the teddy bear firmament. The five enduring teddy designs that stand out are Schuco's Yes/No Bear, Chiltern's Hugmee, Steiff's Original Teddy, Merrythought's Cheeky Bear and Steiff's Zotty, all of which were produced in large numbers over several decades. These teddy bears can frequently be found at specialist bear auctions or among the stock of dealers in vintage bears because, having been manufactured over a long time, they remain in plentiful supply today. However, don't make the mistake of thinking that because they are readily available, they are not worth collecting. In fact, quite the reverse is true since any arctophile building a collection will want to include at least one example of each of these all-time family favorites. Made successful by a combination of good design, high-quality manufacturing and clever marketing, they were winners when they were new and remain so to this day, so it's worth taking a closer look at them individually.

SCHUCO'S YES/NO BEAR

The Schuco Yes/No Bear originated in the 1920s, an era that wholeheartedly embraced novelty and innovation. It was the brainchild of Heinrich Muller, co-founder of a German company called Schreyer & Co that specialised in manufacturing all kinds of mechanical toys, with bears making up just a fraction of the firm's output.

In 1921 Schreyer & Co started to use the trade name Schuco, and shortly afterwards Muller devised the Yes/No mechanism, the name referring to the movements the bear's head could make when its tail was operated. When the tail was moved up and down the bear nodded and when it was moved from side to side, the bear appeared to be shaking its head. The movement was made by a metal rod that ran the length of the bear's body and finished with a ball-and-socket joint in the neck. For children (and adults) who wanted to be able to communicate with their bears, the Yes/No Bear was a magical innovation that proved irresistible.

Yes/No Bears were made in various sizes ranging from very large – 24 in (60 cm) – to downright tiny, as in the case of the 5-inch (12.5-cm) Piccolo Yes/No Bear. They also came in different types and color of mohair, and there was even a Yes/No Clown Bear, produced in the 1930s. As was the case with so many teddy manufacturers, the war put production on hold, but in 1950 the Yes/No Bear was back, with a new name – Tricky – and a slightly new look that included downturned paws and longer legs.

ABOVE: A Yes/No Bear from the 1930s; it measures 19 in (48 cm) and is made from unusual yellow mohair with white tips.

OPPOSITE: A 1950s Yes/No Bear from the Bear Museum at Petersfield in England.

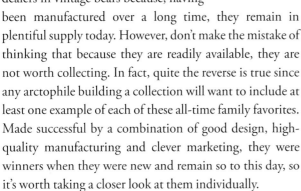

Some delightful Trickys were dressed in traditional German costumes or as schoolchildren, while others had musical mechanisms to add to their novelty value. The range even included a Tricky panda.

CHILTERN'S HUGMEE

Where mechanical ingenuity was the key to the success of Schuco's Yes/No Bear, another favorite that debuted in the 1920s owed its popularity to its extreme huggability. Created by the England-based Chiltern Toy Company in 1923, it remained in production until the firm ceased to exist in the 1960s. There's no denying that Hugmee was a great name for a teddy bear, but there was more to its success than smart marketing. What made it stand out from the many other bears produced at this time was that although its head was stuffed with wood wool (fine wood shavings), its body had a kapok stuffing to make it more cuddly than traditional teds. Early Hugmees did not have permanent, sewn-on labels but they are easy to identify by their vertically stitched noses with raised stitches either side, long arms that dipped at the paws, chunky legs narrowing at the ankles, glass eyes, and claw stitching to paws and feet. They were made from high quality mohair, usually in the normal teddy bear shades but occasionally in brighter hues. Many were fitted with squeakers.

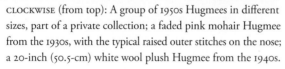

CLOCKWISE (from top): A group of 1950s Hugmees in different sizes, part of a private collection; a faded pink mohair Hugmee from the 1930s, with the typical raised outer stitches on the nose; a 20-inch (50.5-cm) white wool plush Hugmee from the 1940s.

By the time the Second World War started, Chiltern had opened another factory in North London and limited toy production continued here while the Buckinghamshire factory switched to war work. It was at this time that a type of Hugmee known to collectors today as the 'Flat Face' came into production. A shortage of mohair during the war led to the development of this new Hugmee design that required less material than the original because it had a shorter muzzle and stumpier limbs. When the war was over and rationing had ended, Chiltern more or less returned to their original design although the nose lost its distinctive raised outer stitches. Hugmees continued to be made right up until Chiltern was taken over by another company in the 1960s.

BELOW: A trio of 1950s Steiff Original Teddy Bears. The word 'original' was used to remind buyers that the company had invented the jointed bear back in 1902.

The Hugmee is a quintessentially English teddy bear, and its familiarity (it was the childhood bear of many arctophiles born in the post-war period) has made it a firm favorite with British collectors. And then there's that name – who could resist a teddy that demands to be hugged?

STEIFF'S ORIGINAL TEDDY

Steiff began using the word 'original' to describe its teddy bears as early as 1908, in response to the growing number of companies that were jumping on the teddy bear bandwagon. By calling its bears original, the company was reminding people that it had invented the jointed toy bear. As far as most collectors are concerned, however, the name Original Teddy refers to the redesigned teddy bear that Steiff launched in 1950. Out went long muzzles and limbs, and in came fatter stomachs and virtually non-existent humps. Due to its almost cub-like appearance, this was a teddy bear a child could really identify with, and it received an enthusiastic response. Available in just two sizes and two shades of mohair in 1950, by 1951 demand had justified an increase to ten sizes and another two shades of mohair.

The Original Teddy remained unaltered until 1966 when Steiff gave it another make-over. The main change this time affected the bear's face – it is easy to spot post-1966 Original Teddy Bears because they have clipped, heart-shaped muzzles – and this time the hump has gone completely.

With their variations in size, color and style, it would be possible to build up an impressive collection of Original Teddy Bears. Because they were very well made using high quality materials, they tend to age well, and currently they are fairly inexpensive to buy although it is surely only a matter of time before collectors latch on to just how special these bears are.

MERRYTHOUGHT'S CHEEKY BEAR

This highly distinctive teddy bear, with big head, inset velveteen muzzle, wide smile and bells in its ear, was launched by Merrythought in 1956 at the British Toy Fair. Legend has it that the unnamed bear was admired by a royal visitor – some accounts say the Queen, others the Queen Mother – who then declared 'What a cheeky little bear!'

Officially designed by Jean Barber in 1955, Cheeky owed a lot to Punkinhead, an earlier Merrythought design that had been delighting the Canadians since 1948. This early influence was acknowledged by Merrythought in 1986 when they released a Punkinhead lookalike called Ancestor of Cheeky.

The first Cheekys were made in just four sizes, each in various permutations of mohair and artificial silk plush, but when they realised they had a winner on their hands, Merrythought created just about every conceivable

ABOVE: A very early dressed Cheeky Bear, designed by Jean Barber in 1955; this piece was never put into production although a limited edition replica was released in 2006.

OPPOSITE: A post-1966 Original Teddy with its distinctive clipped heart-shaped muzzle.

LEFT: A late 1950s Cheeky, 11 inches (28 cm) tall, made from dark gold mohair.
BELOW: A limited edition Cheeky made to celebrate the Queen's Golden Jubilee in 2002; the golden mohair is sprigged with golden threads.

OPPOSITE: A 2006 replica of a 1950s art silk Cheeky.

variation in order to keep their star bear fresh and interesting. There were Cheekys with open mouths, brightly colored Cheekys, musical Cheekys, dressed 'Twisty' Cheekys and Cheeky pajama cases, for example. As well as using the traditional materials of mohair and art silk, Merrythought pressed new, man-made materials into service, with nylon Cheekys appearing in 1960 and a simulated mink version in 1971. Looking about as far removed from a real bear as possible, Merrythought's Cheeky was pure fun, with his tinkling ears, soft, kapok-stuffed stomach and wildly infectious grin.

When Merrythought made their bid for the collectors' market in the 1990s, it was Cheeky who spearheaded their campaign. He was hugely popular in Japan and the US as well as in his home country, so special limited editions were created to appeal to those markets. Perhaps to help collectors who were running out of display space, a Micro Cheeky that measured just 6 in (15.2 cm) high was introduced in 1994. Merrythought continue to make their Cheeky bears today in ever more inventive designs at their factory in historic Ironbridge in England.

STEIFF'S ZOTTY

Like Merrythought's Cheeky, Steiff's Zotty was a post-war teddy that was designed to have maximum appeal for children. The name derives from the German word *zottig*, which means shaggy, and it is indeed a good description of

the tousle-furred bear. Launched in 1951, Zotty had long, caramel-colored mohair with a lighter tip, and an inset 'bib' of peach-colored mohair. His downturned paws harked back to Teddy Baby, an earlier Steiff creation, and his open mouth gave him a pleasingly eager expression, suggesting that this teddy was all set to play.

Zotty was a massive success story, so successful in fact that Steiff made him in varying styles and sizes right into the 1990s. Other companies also produced Zotty-type bears, a sure sign that Steiff had found a winning formula. Happily for collectors, the genuine article can be distinguished by its peach mohair bib, even if the famous Steiff button-in-ear has been removed.

A Zotty made from white mohair proved less popular than the original, perhaps because the color was none too practical for a child's toy, and so it was produced for just

one year, from 1960 to 1961. Now, of course, this rarer Zotty is sought by collectors while the other varieties that were made in much larger numbers are often overlooked. Zotty deserves greater appreciation, however, because he is a beautifully crafted teddy who in many ways exemplifies the way in which Steiff were moving from their traditional roots into a much more radical direction. Put Zotty side-by-side with Richard Steiff's perfected bear of 1905 and the only similarity is the high quality of the finished product.

ABOVE: A Minky Zotty, 14 in (35 cm) high. This version was made from soft artificial fur between 1969 and 1977.

LEFT: A 20-in (50-cm) Zotty from the late 1950s with working growler, together with a 11-in (28-cm) example from the same period.

This list of all-time family favorites is far from definitive, since many other bears also played a part in establishing the teddy bear as the best-loved children's toy of all time. From the 1920s, Steiff's Petsy with its crazy blue eyes deserves a mention, as do the grumpy-faced Chad Valley Magna from the 1930s, Steiff's adorable Jackie from 1953 and the washable Wendy Boston teddy from 1954. These, and dozens of others, have done their bit to capture the hearts of generations of children. Bears, we salute you!

CLOCKWISE (from top): A typical Wendy Boston-type teddy dating from the late 1950s; a 1930s Chad Valley Magna; in 2006, Steiff launched this limited edition replica of Petsy, an idiosyncratic teddy first produced in 1926; in 1953 Steiff created Jackie to celebrate the 50th anniversary of the teddy bear.

2 WHO AM I?

For decades, Teddy was happy to appear in front of his adoring public with very little on. A nice ribbon tied around the neck was usually the most he went in for, preferring to allow the natural beauty of his mohair to speak for itself. There have been exceptions, of course, such as Steiff's Teddy Clowns which were sold wearing hats and ruffs, and Merrythought's Mr and Mrs Twisty Bear which had clothes sewn onto their bodies. By and large, however, manufacturers left their teddy bears undressed. If their owners wanted them clothed they had to borrow from a doll's wardrobe, persuade a sympathetic grandma to make an outfit, or simply do it themselves. This is precisely what a little girl called Kathleen Phillips did with one of her two

beloved Steiff teddy bears in the era immediately prior to the First World War. Pat, a rare black Steiff, was left undressed but Nora, made from pale blonde mohair, was given a complete outfit including a white wool skirt, white knitted sweater, underwear, boots and even a silk parasol. In a diary entry dated Saturday 12 August 1914, Kathleen writes '…I had a fine game and Pamela came to tea and after we made our teddy bears some clothes.' In May 2001, Pat and Nora were auctioned at Christie's together with their provenance which included Kathleen's nature notebook and many photographs. The collector, teddy bear expert Sue Pearson, subsequently commissioned a wonderful limited edition replica set of Pat and Nora from Steiff.

CLOCKWISE (from above): Kathleen Phillips and her brother, Ivor, playing with Pat and Nora on the beach at Birchington, Kent in 1914; Steiff's Teddy Clowns, circa 1926, which came with hats and neck ruffs; The Twins, British bears by an unknown maker dating from the 1920s – their matching sailor outfits would possibly have been intended for dolls; Merrythought's Mr and Mrs Twisty Bear, 1966, were unusual in that clothing was an integral part of their bodies.

OPPOSITE: Pat (with flag) and Nora today, still sporting the clothes that Kathleen Phillips made for her.

ABOVE (left): During the Second World War, a scarcity of mohair led to many bears being made with sewn-on clothing to disguise the fact that they were mostly fabric and stuffing.
(middle): In the post-war period, Schuco's tiny soccer bears with pipecleaner limbs were very popular.
(right): Maxi, a 1930s Hermann teddy bear, wears knitted lederhosen that are probably original.

DRESSING UP

So dressing a teddy has traditionally been a do-it-yourself option, but recently there has been a trend for teddy bears to adopt the appearance of contemporary personalities and iconic figures, and there is no better way of doing this than dressing up. There's no doubt that the trend has been prompted by demands from the adult collectors' market. In the 1980s, the adult market was in its infancy, with people taking their first tentative steps as teddy bear collectors and still feeling awkward about admitting they had a passion for teddy bears. In this rather hesitant climate, teddy bear makers tended to recycle old designs or come up with new ones that still relied heavily on traditional influences. In the 1990s, however, adult teddy collecting took a giant leap forward, made popular by a number of specialist teddy bear magazines and books, and by a series of sensational teddy auctions that resulted in record prices. Suddenly collecting teddy bears was acceptable, even fashionable, and as word spread manufacturers and artists worked hard to come up with exciting products that would appeal to the new market. The stage was set for the advent of the Lookalike Teddy.

Most arctophiles begin their collections with very traditional teddy bears, perhaps their own childhood bear or one that closely resembles it. They continue along these lines for a little while, adding similar bears until one day they realise that even though they still adore the conventional

teddy, they want to try something else. At this point some might decide to stop collecting teddy bears altogether and switch to egg cups, train sets or whatever, but most are committed collectors who just want bears and bears alone. For them, the only option is to seek out new, distinctive types of teddy, and thanks to the worldwide army of teddy artists and manufacturers, there is no lack of choice. And it is at this point, as they are visiting teddy bear shows and scouring Internet sites in search of innovation, that collectors are ready to fall for the charms of the lookalike.

THE QUEEN AND THE KING

It doesn't take a genius to work out that the more popular a personality, the greater the chance people will want to buy a teddy version. In 2006, the year of Queen Elizabeth II's 80th birthday, various manufacturers brought out tribute bears that were clearly meant to represent the Queen of England. For example, the English firm Merrythought created a regal-looking bear dressed in ceremonial garter robes and wearing a specially commissioned Order of the Garter brooch. The implication is that the piece is a teddy representation of Her Majesty but perhaps to avoid any royal displeasure, it is tactfully called the Queen's 80th Birthday Bear. Similarly, the New Zealand teddy bear designer and manufacturer Robin Rive created an attractive teddy dressed in the sort of outfit Her Majesty wears when performing one of her daytime engagements. Dressed in a smart pink coat and hat and carrying a matching handbag, the bear is called Ma'am, suggesting rather than asserting that it's an affectionate representation of the Queen.

ABOVE: Ma'am, a limited edition teddy created by New Zealand's Robin Rive to mark the Queen's 80th birthday.

RIGHT: Queen's 80th Birthday Bear, a Merrythought limited edition teddy bear showing Her Majesty in ceremonial regalia.

For all this careful skirting around when it comes to naming lookalike teddy bears, some designers are happy to boldly declare the inspiration for their creations, whether the figure in question is living or dead. Certainly when the artist behind the Bear Island name created a prototype teddy inspired by Elvis Presley, she had no qualms about calling her brilliant bear Elvis. Similarly, when Robin Rive created a teddy to celebrate the 70th birthday of opera legend Luciano Pavarotti in 2005, she made her intention plain by naming it after him. When the figure in question is fictional, however, the thorny issues of copyright and licensing come into play,

leaving designers intent on creating tribute bears with no choice but to choose an alternative name for their pieces. So you have the maker of a wonderful James Bond-inspired teddy bear calling her piece Triple-O-Seven, and the artist responsible in 1998 for creating a superb pair with an uncanny resemblance to Wallace and Gromit chose to sell them as Willis and Grimmit. In a sensible world, one-off artist interpretations of well-known fictional characters should not incur the wrath of corporate copyright, but stranger things have happened. The artists in question are well advised to proceed with care.

ABOVE: Willis and Grimmit bear a striking resemblance to a well-known animated duo.
RIGHT: Pavarotti, created by Robin Rive in 2005 to mark the opera singer's 70th birthday; the bear is undressed so only his name links him to his famous namesake.

OPPOSITE (left): Elvis, created as a prototype design by Bear Island.
(right): Triple-O-Seven. 'The name's Bear … James Bear'.

THE ULTIMATE SANTA

One character that can be represented in teddy form without fear of a writ is Santa Claus. As an individual responsible for giving untold thousands of teddy bears to well-behaved and grateful children, it's entirely fitting that he should be interpreted as a teddy himself on many occasions. Outstanding Belgian artist Helga Torfs created what has to be the ultimate Santa Ted, complete with red suit trimmed with white fur and a white beard skilfully applied to his brown mohair face. Halloween also inspires its fair share of lookalike teddy bears. Although the pagan origins of Halloween are largely overlooked these days, it's a time for children to have fun, dress up as ghosts and witches, and of course, go trick or treating. Not to be outdone, the teddy bear frequently gets in on the act, appearing with a pointy black hat and orange accessories – following the general theme without ever looking threatening. That's one thing a teddy can never be.

Finally, with some novelty teddy bears you'd be better to ask the question 'What am I?' rather than 'Who am I?' The US-based Boyds company hit on a crafty way to make vegetables more appealing to children by creating an ingenious range of Vegetable Patch bears. This healthy range featured bears dressed up as eggplants, tomatoes, carrots and peas. The teddy has enjoyed many adventures since it was invented in 1902, but it's probably unlikely that Richard Steiff ever thought there'd be a vegetable interpretation of his jointed toy bear!

LEFT: Hermann Teddy Original's 2005 Halloween Bear.
ABOVE: A teddy disguised in a peapod, from Boyds' Vegetable Patch collection.

OPPOSITE: Santa Claus, as interpreted by Belgian bear artist Helga Torfs.

The teddy bear's iconic status has led to its adoption as a lovable mascot by hundreds of very different organizations. The first time teddy was used was just a year or so after his invention when he was used in the campaign to get Theodore Roosevelt re-elected as President. Small teddy bears were given away to Roosevelt's supporters and today these items are highly prized by collectors. Having succeeded in getting the President back into office, the teddy wisely withdrew from the political field and turned his considerable talents to promoting both charitable and commercial endeavours.

As a figurehead, the teddy has notched up considerable success representing such diverse subjects as European cities, major sporting events and even a long-running campaign against forest fires. The latter started in August

ABOVE (left): Smokey Bear, a limited edition teddy designed by Bev White for Cooperstown Bears.
(right): Replica by Robin Rive of the teddy given to Roosevelt's supporters during his re-election campaign.

1944 when the US Co-operative Forest Fire Prevention Program launched Smokey Bear as its official mascot. Earlier that year a poster featuring Walt Disney's Bambi had been used to drive home the message about the danger of forest fires, but although the poster was a success, Bambi had only been on temporary loan from Disney. For a permanent mascot, the Forest Service needed to create their very own character and they decided that a bear was the best possible choice. In order to give him maximum appeal, they softened up Smokey's appearance considerably. Even on his very first poster he was depicted as round and cuddly, with big eyes and a gentle, intelligent expression – exactly like a teddy bear, in fact. The addition of blue trousers, a hat and a spade completed his transformation from genuine bear to teddy mascot.

REAL-LIFE DRAMA

In an interesting twist in which life followed art, some six years after Smokey's creation a real bear cub survived a horrific blaze in the Lincoln National Forest near Capitan, New Mexico. The little bear was injured but miraculously survived and was taken to safety. Having recovered from his burns, he was taken to live at the National Zoo in Washington DC where he came to symbolise all that Smokey stands for, and many people mistakenly believe he was the original inspiration behind Smokey Bear. His ordeal touched the hearts of the American people and over the years he was visited at the zoo by thousands of adoring fans. When he died in 1976, he was buried in the Smokey Bear State Park in Capitan, his place of origin.

Today every child in America is familiar with Smokey's 'Only You Can Prevent Forest Fires' catchphrase, and it would be possible to fill an entire museum with the various Smokey posters, books, toys and other bits of ephemera that have been produced over the years. Of most interest to teddy collectors are the various plush Smokey Bears that have been in constant production since the early 1950s. Leading manufacturers such as Ideal, Knickerbocker and Dakin have all created their own versions but the most interesting in recent years has to be the limited edition Smokey designed by leading US bear artist Beverly White for Cooperstown Bears.

THE BERLINER BEAR

Another example of bear-turned-teddy turns up in the German capital of Berlin which has been associated with the bear for over 700 years. The martial bear that is shown in profile on the city's flag has been reinterpreted as a soft teddy wearing crown and sash, and for decades visitors to Berlin have been able to take these small cuddly mascots home as souvenirs. For the most part they are cheap and cheerful, but there are a few notable exceptions. The German manufacturer Schuco made tiny jointed Berliner

Berliner Bear – a collectable souvenir of the German capital.

months to perfect his design of a smiling, teddy-ish bear wearing a belt of the five interlocking Olympic rings. It was worth the effort – Misha was produced by Dakin in plush, ceramic, plastic, wood, glass and metal, and became the most successful sporting mascot ever in commercial terms. Even today it is hard to think of any mascot that has come close to rivalling his success – quite ironic considering Misha was the product of a fiercely anti-capitalist regime.

LEFT: The gentle smiling face of this Bruges Bear makes him more teddy than bear.
BELOW: Misha, the Moscow Olympics mascot, produced by Dakin in 1980.

OPPOSITE: Pudsey, the official mascot of Children in Need, sold under licence by The Bear Factory in 2004.

Bears that are very collectable today, and Steiff have produced some really lovely examples including a brown mohair one, made between 1993 and 1994 and featuring jointed arms and legs. Other European cities that have historic associations with the bear, such as Berne in Switzerland and Bruges in Belgium, also make good use of teddy bears as souvenirs.

These days it seems that every major sporting event has an official mascot representing the spirit of the occasion and, more cynically, to generate income from sales of licensed merchandise. When the Olympic Games went to Moscow in 1980, the Soviet Union chose a bear called Misha as their mascot. It was an unsurprising choice since Russia has been called 'The Bear' by the rest of the world for centuries, and Misha is a traditional Russian nickname for a bear. The Olympic Misha was developed by Victor Chizikov, an illustrator of children's books who took six

PUDSEY – A TRUE TEDDY HERO

The mascot teddy bears featured so far in this chapter started out as bears but evolved into teddy bears in order to achieve a wider appeal. They keep some bear-like features to remind people of their origins – a heraldic symbol in the case of the Berliner Bear, and Smokey's visual link with real animals potentially endangered by man's carelessness. In these cases even a limited sense of realism is enough, but when it comes to teddy mascots created from imagination, no such reference is necessary. So, when the BBC tasked designer Joanna Ball with creating a teddy bear to be the official logo of their Children in Need charity, she was able to ignore genuine ursine characteristics in preference for something with mass visual appeal. Pudsey Bear, named after the designer's home town of Pudsey in Yorkshire, is a bright sunshine yellow, with a white and red-spotted bandage over one eye to empathise with the children he represents, and a big smile to dispel any unease. Launched on the 1985 Children in Need telethon, Pudsey has appeared on every successive annual show and his image has adorned cracker boxes, soap, mugs, mobile phone covers and literally dozens of other items. He is a true teddy hero, turning up at every Children in Need fundraiser held up and down the UK and generating millions of pounds for his charity through the sales of Pudsey merchandise.

This special ability of the teddy bear to generate income has not escaped the notice of the world's advertising fraternity. Since their creation in 1902, countless bears have been used as product mascots or in ad campaigns, and some arctophiles base their entire collections on these promotional teddy bears. Among the most famous promotional teddy bears is a soft white bear called Snuggle which can be found all over the world representing a Lever Bros fabric softener. The product has different names in different countries – in Belgium and Holland it is Robintje, Germany and Austria know it as Kuschelweich, it is Snuggles in the USA and the Spanish call it Mimosin. Snuggle has been produced by various firms including Russ and Gund and although slight design differences occur from maker to maker, it remains essentially the same teddy every time. In Germany, the condensed milk sold under the Baerenmarke label has featured teddy-like bears on its packaging since the early part of the 20th century and more recently it has been possible to purchase very cute Baerenmarke teddy bears made from plush. Other products promoted by teddy bears at one time or another include Bear Brand hosiery, Pampers diapers, Haribo confectionery, Charmin toilet paper, Pom-Bears potato snack, Pustefix (a German bubble mix), Gummi Bears and even Coca Cola, if polar bears can be extended into the teddy bear family.

CLOCKWISE (from top left): Lever Brothers' Snuggle; Pampi Bear, a promotional teddy for Pampers diapers, created by Steiff; the Charmin toilet paper teddy.

OPPOSITE: Haribo Gold Bear, a jointed mohair teddy made by Steiff in a limited edition of 5000 in 2003.

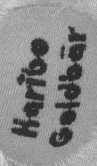

BEAM ME UP, TEDDY

Even organizations that do not have an official teddy mascot see the benefit of selling bears in order to generate extra income. For example, at Raymond Blanc's Michelin-starred restaurant Le Manoir aux Quat'Saisons in England, diners can buy a souvenir teddy dressed in chef's whites, with the restaurant's name and owner's signature printed on the front, to remind them of their delightful culinary experience. Similarly, at the 'Star Trek: The Experience' attraction in Las Vegas in 2005, thrilled Trekkies could buy a plush Starfleet Bear dressed in the uniform of a Star Trek, The Next Generation™ crew member. There is no connection whatsoever between the evergreen sci-fi series and the teddy bear except, perhaps, the fact that both have millions of fans the world over. The truth is that no other toy comes anywhere near rivalling the teddy as a figurehead, and it's not hard to understand why marketing people return to it time and again. It appeals to both sexes, is instantly evocative of comfort and security, and as the examples shown in this chapter demonstrate, it is endlessly versatile, changing its appearance to look fresh and attractive with each new role. No wonder Teddy is the world's favorite mascot.

RIGHT: Starfleet Bear, purchased at a Star Trek tourist attraction in Las Vegas.

OPPOSITE: A Le Manoir aux Quat'Saisons teddy bear.

How much would you be prepared to pay for a collectable teddy? While the vast majority of bears are fairly reasonable, some have sold in recent years for an awful lot of money. Strange really, because for most teddy collectors, a bear's monetary value is irrelevant. What matters is the thrill of the chase, the sheer pleasure of getting hold of a rare, interesting or beautiful teddy to add to a collection. Few true collectors think in terms of investment or profit, which is just as well because the value of antiques and collectables is notoriously fickle. Objects that set record saleroom prices one year can fall from favor the next and it's as true of teddy bears as any other item, so trying to make money from them is a risky business. Having said that, a handful of ultra-special bears are so desirable that their owners could name a six-figure sum and still have a dozen eager buyers lining up with check books in hand. The original Winnie the Pooh, perhaps the most famous teddy of all time, spends his retirement years on display in the New York Public Library and is unlikely ever to be sold, but if he did come onto the market, he would almost certainly break all previous auction records because of his status as an international superstar. This chapter looks at some of the extraordinary prices paid for some teddy bears over the last 20 years, and examines what has made them so special.

BEAR FOR A PRINCESS

In 1989, a rare red Steiff bear called Alfonzo made teddy history when he sold at Christie's in London for the record price of $23,080. While this might seem a bit tame by today's standards, back then it was an extraordinary amount of money to pay for a teddy bear. But buying Alfonzo proved to be an extremely clever move on the part of his new owner, Ian Pout.

Mr Pout was in the vanguard of the collectable teddy bear movement. In 1985 he opened Teddy Bears of Witney, the UK's first shop to specialize in selling new and old teddy bears. He had originally sold antiques from his shop in the pretty Oxfordshire town but bears gradually began to take over until they became the focus of his business. When a postcard promoting a sale at Christie's arrived in the shop one day, Mr Pout was intrigued when he read a riddle on the reverse of the card. 'When is a red teddy bear white?' it asked. 'When it belonged to a Russian princess,' followed the reply. On the front of the card, Mr Pout saw a photograph of Alfonzo, a slightly worn red Steiff teddy wearing some kind of costume.

Already half under the bear's spell, Mr Pout went to the sale where he saw Alfonzo properly for the first time and became even more smitten. Not only did this teddy have immense visual charm, it had the most wonderful provenance imaginable. Alfonzo had been a gift in 1908 (further proof that Steiff was experimenting with colour at this time) from Grand Duke George Michailovich, a cousin of Tsar Nicholas II, to his little daughter, Princess Xenia. The outfit worn by Alfonzo was a Cossack costume, made from cotton sateen by Xenia's English nanny. The Russian princess adored her bear and took it with her when she visited her royal relatives at Buckingham Palace in 1914. War broke out soon after she arrived and so Xenia remained in England, escaping the sad fate of most of her family, including her beloved father, who were murdered by the Russian revolutionaries. Having lost her father, Xenia treasured her red teddy more than ever as it was the only gift from him that she had taken with her to England. Princess Xenia married an American in 1921 and moved to Long Island, taking Alfonzo with her, of course. When the

Alfonzo, arguably the most romantic bear in teddy history.

Princess died in 1965, Alfonzo lived with her daughter before arriving at Christie's in 1989.

For Christie's, setting a realistic estimate for Alfonzo proved difficult. Expectations were high due to his romantic history coupled with his rarity (he was a model never commercially produced by Steiff) but nobody knew how much anyone would be prepared to pay for him. The catalogue gave an estimate of $3,800–$5,700 but some of the prospective buyers had deep pockets and the bidding quickly went past $16,800, the previous saleroom record for a teddy bear, set at Sotheby's in 1987 for a rare, white, muzzled Steiff. In spite of this, Mr Pout held his nerve and finally secured Alfonzo for $22,090.

Since that exhilarating moment of auction history, Alfonzo has become world famous as the signature bear for Teddy Bears of Witney. His portrait hangs over the shop's entrance and once inside, visitors are able to see him and pay their respects. Mr Pout commissioned an exclusive full-size limited edition replica from Steiff, so visitors could buy a piece of the Alfonzo magic to take away with them, but these new bears have long since sold out. Now, Alfonzo fans can buy a small-scale replica called Baby Alfonzo, true to the original in every way except size. Alfonzo is a teddy bear legend and nobody knows how much he would sell for if he was auctioned today – but one thing's for sure, it would be many times more than $23,090!

THE COLONEL'S BEAR
Following Alfonzo's memorable auction, prices for rare old teddy bears started to rise steeply but it wasn't until 1994 that they broke the six-figure barrier. The teddy achieving this remarkable feat runs Alfonzo a very close second in most arctophiles' hearts. Called Teddy Girl, this beautiful 1904 Steiff teddy was highly desirable because of her cinnamon-colored mohair which is favored by collectors, and because she is a rare center seam bear. Steiff center seam bears have heads made from two pieces of mohair that are joined in the center – the object being to make as many bears as possible from one width of mohair. Her added attraction, however, was that she had been the childhood teddy of Colonel Bob Henderson, a Second World War veteran and one of the world's best-known collectors. He did much work for charity and helped popularize teddy bear collecting for adults, so there was great excitement in the crowded salerooms when Teddy Girl came under the hammer at Christie's in December 1994. After a fierce tussle she sold for an astounding $209,870 to Mr Yoshihiro Sekiguchi of the Japanese Sun Arrow toy company. Teddy Girl is now seeing out her old age at the Izu Teddy Bear Museum in Japan where she has many other gorgeous bears to keep her company.

RIGHT: Baby Alfonzo, a small scale replica of Alfonzo made by Steiff in a limited. edition of 5,000. The bears were produced exclusively for Teddy Bears of Witney.

OPPOSITE: Teddy Girl, the lifelong companion of teddy collector Colonel Bob Henderson.

TALE OF THE *TITANIC* TEDS

Some historic events remain in the public consciousness long after they happen, a tragic example being the sinking of the *Titanic* in 1912, which even today continues to hold a unique fascination. Any teddy that has even a loose connection with the stricken White Star liner is bound to have mass appeal. Steiff created 494 black 'mourning' teddy bears for the British market shortly after the disaster, and whenever one of these appears on the market, collectors compete to own them. When Sotheby's auctioned a very fine example in 1990, Ian Pout, the successful bidder, paid over $45,770 in order to take the rare bear called Othello

back to Witney. A decade later, when another of the black bears came up for sale at Christie's, the price was even more extraordinary. This particular example created a stir because of his fine condition – apparently his original owner had not cared much about him and had relegated him to the back of the wardrobe, preserving him beautifully. Apart from a small hole in one footpad and a slight thinning of the fur on his head, he looked almost pristine. His great condition together with the craze for all things *Titanic*, led Christie's teddy bear specialist Daniel Agnew to predict an exciting sale. The catalogue estimate for the bear was $28,600–$38,000 but Daniel was quietly confident it

LEFT: Othello, Ian Pout's beautiful black Steiff teddy bear.

OPPOSITE: A black *Titanic* teddy bear, sold at Christie's South Kensington in December 2000.

RIGHT: The limited edition Steiff teddy which sold for
a new world record price of $247,000, following some
fancy accessorising by Louis Vuitton.

OPPOSITE: Steiff's remarkable 125 Karat teddy bear.

RIGHT: The limited edition Steiff teddy which sold for
a new world record price of $247,000, following some
fancy accessorising by Louis Vuitton.

OPPOSITE: Steiff's remarkable 125 Karat teddy bear.

would reach more than this, although even he was unprepared for the result. As it was, the bear's condition, rarity and the *Titanic* association combined to create the biggest saleroom sensation since Teddy Girl's moment of glory in 1994. After some frantic bidding between a telephone bidder and someone in the saleroom, the hammer came down at over $173,550 (buyer's premium included) and a new record had been set for one of the *Titanic* bears. Don't assume though that this is the going rate for all 1912 *Titanic* teddy bears – prices are affected by many different factors including their condition and the general state of the economy.

TEDDIES 2000
Desirable as old teddies are, they are not the only ones to sell for sensational prices. In recent years modern teds have been catching up with their vintage cousins. Indeed, a bear made in 2000 currently holds the record for the highest price paid at auction for a teddy. This was no ordinary auction, though; Les Teddies de l'An 2000 was held in Monaco in aid of the charity Monaco Aide et Présence (MAP) which works to improve

children's lives in the developing world. Margarete Steiff GmbH, as part of its program of charitable initiatives, produced a limited edition of 40 teddy bears to be sold on behalf of MAP. The bears were then given to some of the fashion world's most prestigious names including Balmain, Cartier and Christian Dior, who styled and dressed them individually. They were then sold at a glamorous auction attended by Crown Prince Albert of Monaco, the Honorary Chairman of MAP. Thanks in part to its high-profile patron, Les Teddies de l'An 2000 was attended by wealthy, fashion-conscious society figures as well as dedicated Steiff collectors, so the stage was set for some animated bidding. Add to this the phenomenon known to seasoned buyers as 'auction fever' that compels unwary bidders to carry on way beyond their intended limit, and it is easy to see how some impressive sums of money could be raised for a good cause.

Even so, when the stylish Louis Vuitton bear came under the hammer, nobody was expecting it to set a new world record. Mr Jesse Kim, a Korean businessman who made his considerable fortune in the toy manufacturing industry, paid a mind-boggling $247,000 for it. A great admirer of Louis Vuitton products, Mr Kim discovered a bear he just could not resist. In the face of some serious opposition, he simply kept bidding. The following spring, the Jeju Teddy Bear Museum in Korea opened, featuring the Louis Vuitton bear as one of its prize exhibits.

More recently, another limited edition Steiff teddy has been setting collectors' hearts a-flutter in a similar manner.

The 125 Karat teddy bear was produced in 2005 to mark the 125th anniversary of the founding of the Steiff company. A teddy with more more jewelry than a rap star, it was marketed with the line 'Only the best is good enough for this anniversary', which neatly paraphrases Margarete Steiff's opinion that 'Only the best is good enough for our children'.

Set in 18 carat yellow gold, the 125 Karat teddy's eyes are made of two sapphire cabochons and surrounded by 20 diamonds.

ONLY THE BEST

So what exactly is 'the best'? Well, there are several different elements to the edition. The bear itself is an opulent feast for the eye, made from the finest mohair combined with raw silk to achieve a unique sheen, and with additional glittering gold threads hand-knotted into the soft fur. The process of creating this special mohair was so labor-intensive that it took 20 hours to make just one meter of it, at a cost, apparently, of $1,600 per meter. Such a dazzling mohair deserves equally dazzling eyes, so the 125 Karat teddy looks out from two cabochon sapphires, each surrounded by 20 Russian cut diamonds and set in 18 carat gold. The bear's molded nose and mouth are cast in 24 carat gold, as is its button-in-ear and the medallion it wears around its neck.

Pretty impressive stuff, but that's far from all. To keep the 125 Karat teddy company, it comes with a bejewelled replica of Margarete Steiff's first elephant pin cushion, and both pieces are supplied in a purpose-built, lockable presentation case. In that case, there's a drawer containing a booklet about the

The 125 Karat teddy's nose and mouth are worked in pure
24 carat gold.

special edition, a Mont Blanc fountain pen and a bottle of
gold ink. The icing on the cake for purchasers comes in the
guise of a luxury trip to Germany to collect the set, during
which they enjoy a special tour of The World of Steiff and
Margarete Steiff's birthplace, a celebratory dinner and a peek
at the company's zealously guarded archives. All this for 25,000
Euros ($32,000), which makes the 125 Karat teddy bear the
most expensive limited edition teddy bear ever produced. Not
a bargain, perhaps, but for those who like to flash the cash, it's
definitely something to get the neighbors round for.

In the 20 years or so that have passed since teddy bear
collecting became recognized as a hobby, many wonderful
bears have been sold for very large sums of money. Most of
these record-breaking bears, however, have been vintage ones,
with just a few modern exceptions. This is a great shame since
contemporary bears can be every bit as impressive as their
senior relatives, especially those made by teddy bear artists.
It's high time that artist-made bears deserved recognition as
true works of art, and if recent events from Down Under are
anything to go by, this change could be imminent.

THE MASTER PAINTER

Australian artist Lisa Rosenbaum is an exceptional teddy bear artist who trades as the Oz Matilda Bears Co. In November 2003, she listed on ebay an exquisite 26-in (66-cm) teddy called The Master Painter that she had hand-painted in oils. Although she loves oil painting, it was the first time Lisa had combined the medium with her bears, and the result was unlike anything collectors had seen before, combining teddy bear artistry with fine art. Reaction was enthusiastic almost to the point of hysteria – The Master Painter received 62 bids from Europe, Japan, Australia and the US. When bidding closed it was sold for a staggering $17,700 to a Mrs Ann Kelly from Ireland – a confirmed world record price for any bear artist creation sold either privately or at auction. Amazingly, just the previous day, the same purchaser had paid $15,100 for another fabulous artist bear, this time a piece called Captain Nemo, created by the multi-talented US artist Michelle Lamb.

Whether vintage or contemporary, it seems that one of the teddy bear's most remarkable achievements has been to remain a much-loved children's toy while simultaneously becoming a highly prized artifact on the collectables market. Performing such an unlikely double act presents no problem whatsoever to the master of disguise.

RIGHT: The Master Painter by Lisa Rosenbaum of the Oz Matilda Bears Co. set a new world record price for an artist-made teddy bear.

OPPOSITE: Michelle Lamb's Captain Nemo sold for $15,100 on ebay.

A teddy bear's main priority is to deliver unconditional companionship to its owner, and most of them are happy to do this by being available for hugging whenever required. Participation in gentle activities such as tea parties may also be called for and sometimes, children being what they are, a certain amount of boisterous play might arise. Many a teddy has sustained injuries in the course of an over-enthusiastic game of make-believe, but such wounds are borne with pride since teddy bears know that, by and large, the better condition the bear, the less its child owner has been interested in it.

Not all teddy bears, however, find the role of huggable playmate rewarding, and so they have another purpose. This is especially true of bears targeted at an adult market because people who are uncomfortable with the idea of owning a teddy for sentimental reasons often find a functional bear more acceptable. This is not to say that secondary-function bears are the sole preserve of the adult market – throughout teddy history there have been many instances of dual purpose children's bears – but it is undeniable that adults find the concept of a useful teddy bear particularly appealing.

LEFT: A Steiff Hot Water Bottle Bear, circa 1907, which sold at Christie's for $62,800 in December 2002.

OPPOSITE: Book-ends decorated with plush bears that have been stuck on; however charming they are, they fail the dual purpose test as they cannot be removed from the bookends and played with.

MULTI-TALENTED TEDS

Over the years the teddy's form has been pressed into service, becoming useful objects such as muffs, book-ends, backpacks and handbags to name just a few. But unless the object can stand alone as a teddy, it cannot be called genuinely dual purpose. For example, two plush teddy bears glued to a pair of wooden bookends cannot be removed to be hugged or played with. They therefore fail to fulfil the teddy's primary function and so cannot be called dual purpose. On the other hand, a tiny jointed

mohair teddy which doubles as a scent bottle can be played with and cuddled, and because it also has a practical application it qualifies where the book-ends fail.

One of the first dual purpose teddy bears to be created was Steiff's Hot Water Bottle Bear, a gorgeous 20-in (51-cm) blond mohair teddy with a cavity into which a canister filled with hot water could be inserted. The bear was then laced up to keep the canister safe inside. It was launched in 1907, a year in which Steiff made an unprecedented 975,000 bears but although the company was riding high, the Hot Water

Bottle Bear received a chilly reaction from the public – even though demand should have been high after the bitter temperatures experienced the previous winter. It may have been a case of too much novelty too soon, or perhaps parents were concerned about the possibility of their children being scalded, although the tight seal on the water canister should have allayed these fears. For whatever reason, only 90 Hot Water Bottle Bears were created during the seven years of their production. Ironically, this early 20th-century flop has become a massive hit 100 years later. In 2001, Steiff produced a replica Hot Water Bottle Bear in a limited edition of 3,000 and demand for it was so high that the edition sold out rapidly. Then, in December 2002, an original Hot Water Bottle Bear was sold at the 100 Years of the Teddy Bear Sale at Christie's South Kensington saleroom for $62,800 against an estimate of $28,600–$38,000. It is possible that the publicity surrounding the recent replica helped secure this exceptional amount, but the fact that the bear retained its original canister is a more likely explanation, since it's believed to be the only one outside the Steiff archive to do so.

ONE FOR THE BABIES ...

While the secondary purpose of Steiff's Hot Water Bottle Bear was to warm cold children, their Rattle Bear was designed to amuse and distract their baby brothers and sisters. Made from around 1912, these charming little chaps measured about 5¹/₂ in (14 cm) high and were available in white or golden mohair. Although the latter color was the more sensible option for a child's toy, it has to be said that the white mohair really suited these little gems. An upturned face and small glass eyes (which wouldn't have a hope of passing our stringent modern safety standards)

lent them a certain magic, and their crowning glory was the tiny metal rattle concealed in their tummies.

Steiff Rattle Bears are in demand with collectors because examples in good condition are few and far between. One suffering extensive damage came up for auction at Christie's South Kensington saleroom in London in July 2006, with a miniature Schuco Yes/No teddy in the same lot. Despite the poor condition of both items, the hammer went down on $760 against an estimate of $380–$570, proving that for some collectors, sheer charm can compensate for serious flaws. In the museum at Teddy Bears of Witney, in the UK, an original Steiff Rattle Bear in much better condition can be seen. The shop launched a limited edition replica in 2005 that

RIGHT: The 1912 Steiff Rattle Bear, owned by Teddy Bears of Witney, side-by-side with the shop's 2005 replica of it.

OPPOSITE: A Steiff replica Hot Water Bottle Bear from 2001.

was faithful in almost every detail, while Steiff North America offered a 10-in (25.5 cm) white Rattle Bear in their 2006 collection.

Over the years many other manufacturers have produced teddy bears with rattles inside. An unjointed example measuring 10 in (25.5 cm) high was made in blue and white artificial silk plush by an unknown maker in the 1950s. Although it's not particularly high quality, its head and upper body wobble frantically when the bear is shaken and it's easy to appreciate the delight this would have given a small child. More recently, teddy stars from popular books and TV shows have been widely available with rattles inside, including Winnie the Pooh, Paddington, Forever Friends and the Care Bears.

PAJAMA STUFFING

In searching for secondary uses for their teddy bears, manufacturers have made good use of the old adage, 'A place for everything, and everything in its place'. The obvious place for a child's nightclothes is on the bed, and since this is also where teddy is likely to be, what could be more sensible than a teddy bear pajama case? The English manufacturer Merrythought has been a big fan of this practical idea, and has produced a large number of teddy bedtime clothes cases over the years. Some of these fail the dual purpose test as they are more bedtime clothes case than teddy (as in the case of the Pooh-in-bed sachet produced in 1967) but the Cheeky nightdress case launched in the same year fits the bill, it can be hugged and played with like a normal teddy as long as its inner pocket is full. The example illustrated (right) measures 26 in (66 cm) high and is made from golden mohair with a pink quilted satin inner pocket; he lost one of his ears some time ago but his owner likes to keep him just the way he is. Lots of other firms also made

CLOCKWISE (from top): 1960s Cheeky bedtime clothes case from Merrythought – front view; back of the 1960s Cheeky bedtime clothes case, showing the zip-up compartment; Pooh-in-bed sachet by Merrythought – it can't be played with as a teddy so is not dual purpose.

OPPOSITE: A 1950s artificial silk plush Rattle Bear, maker unknown.

bedtime clothes case teddy bears. One rather charming 1940s or 1950s example by an unidentified maker features a mother bear holding her little cub. The mother wears a long, pink gingham dress that conceals the fact she doesn't have any legs. Instead, an opening in her dress reveals the perfect place for storing a nightie or pajamas.

Continuing with the bedtime theme, one ingenious manufacturer produced a glow-in-the-dark bear, designed to provide a little reassuring light for children afraid of the dark. Made from mid-brown mohair, the 11-in (28-cm) teddy has luminous vinyl pads that glow when the light is turned off. Dating from the late 1950s, the identity of the bear's maker is uncertain but most experts believe it to be Blue Ribbon Playthings, as the same design minus the glow-in-the-dark feature has been

found on bears that have been positively identified as theirs. Today his rather ghostly glow lasts for just three or four minutes, scarcely enough time for a child to fall asleep, but it might have lasted longer when he was new.

HEAVEN SCENT

Perhaps the best known of all vintage dual purpose teddy bears are the miniature bears created by Schuco in the 1920s. Created in jewel-bright shades as well as the more muted golden mohair, they were *de rigueur* for every quirkily fashionable young lady of the era. Schuco was renowned for its mechanical toys and the firm used its expertise to produce metal-framed novelty bears between 3.5 and 6 in (9 and 15.5 cm) high. They were covered with short-pile mohair plush and concealed powder compacts, lipstick holders, scent

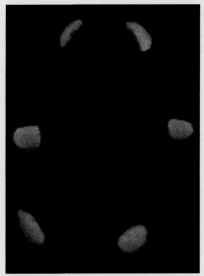

CLOCKWISE (from top left): A 1950s glow-in-the-dark teddy bear; a Glow-in-the-dark teddy at night; this $3^{1}/_{2}$-in (9-cm) green mohair Schuco teddy bear has a secret … it opens to reveal a powder puff and lipstick.

OPPOSITE: A mother-and-baby bedtime clothes case teddy.

bottles and so on. There was even one that contained three 'lucky' dice which were perhaps intended for gambling, but were more likely regarded as good luck charms. Schuco found yet another ingenious use for their little teddy bears when they devised a 5-in (14-cm) bicycle clip. All these items are popular with collectors but they prefer examples in tip-top condition – so scent bottles lacking cork stoppers and compacts with broken hinges will not be as sought-after as those in full working order.

In recent years, new technology has brought a number of techno-teds onto the market but few have found a lasting place in our affections. The main exception to this is Teddy Ruxpin, a story-telling bear who was considered the height of innovation when launched in 1985. A happy-looking teddy who appealed to children, Teddy Ruxpin could talk, thanks to story cassettes inserted into a tape player in his back. Better still, his eyes and mouth moved

ABOVE: A 5-in (12-cm) lilac mohair Schuco scent bottle teddy bear with boot button eyes.
BELOW: The same bear with its head removed to access the scent bottle.

OPPOSITE: The story-telling Teddy Ruxpin.

in perfect sync with the story he was telling. Children adored him, and parents appreciated the helping paw he lent them when introducing their children to the joy of books. For a couple of years Teddy Ruxpin was huge, but as sophisticated electronic toys took over he gradually disappeared from the toyshops. In 2006 he returned, upgraded to use digital technology and with large, child-friendly operating buttons, but otherwise essentially the same old Teddy Ruxpin. He looks nothing like the first Steiff teddy bears who are his distant ancestors, but it's likely that the endlessly inventive Richard Steiff would have approved of him. Teddy Ruxpin earns his dual purpose status by bringing joy to children and at the same time encouraging them to read.

"Riding on trains quite new to bears,
And counting money to pay their fares."

Bears had featured in children's literature long before the arrival of the teddy bear, in folk tales that had been passed on from one generation to the next. Unlike the spate of teddy bear stories that appeared after 1903, however, these tales for the most part involved bears being aggressive, foolish or both. In *The Wren and the Bear*, for example, the bear's remarks about the wren's chicks sparks all-out warfare between four-footed beasts and birds, while in *The Battle of the Beasts*, a bear is terrified and defeated by a domestic cat. Even in Goldilocks and the Three Bears, the best known of all bear folk tales, the ursine family get angry when they discover Goldilocks in their house (at least in the stories published before political correctness determined that the bears should make friends with their intruder). This unsympathetic treatment of bears in folk tales is not surprising given that they posed a genuine danger to people living in some remote rural areas. Along with wolves, bears were the bogeymen of children's nightmares and threats of being taken by them were used to browbeat youngsters into good behavior.

That all changed when the stuffed and jointed bear burst onto the toy scene. Now the bear was immortalized in print as a friendly, cuddly creature, occasionally mischievous but never malicious. This new persona had everything to do with the teddy, and hardly anything at all to do with the bear, even though one of the very first stories of the bear as a lovable character featured 'teddy bears' that were remarkably bear-like. The Roosevelt Bears – Teddy B and Teddy G – were created by Canadian-born Seymour Eaton in a series of verses he wrote for the *Ladies Home Journal* and which later appeared in various leading American newspapers. The success of Teddy B and Teddy G led to a number of books about their adventures, the first of which, *The Roosevelt Bears: Their Travels and Adventures*, was published in 1905.

LEFT: Bears frequently feature in old folk tales, almost always in an unflattering light.

OPPOSITE: Winnie-the-Pooh produced by Hermann Teddy Original.

A BEAR CALLED POOH

Popular as they were in their day, The Roosevelt Bears failed to find fame outside the arctophile scene, but no bear from a book has found more success than Winnie-the-Pooh. An enormous worldwide hit when he debuted in the 1920s, A.A. Milne's 'bear of little brain' has retained his popularity to this day, due in large part to the whimsical charm of his personality, but helped along by the relentless marketing of the Disney corporation which obtained Pooh's film and merchandising rights in 1961. It has been estimated that Pooh is more valuable to Disney than Mickey, Donald and Goofy combined, although purists

argue that Disney's Pooh has little or nothing in common with Milne's original character.

The real Winnie-the-Pooh was a teddy bear made by the Farnell firm, bought in 1921 from Harrods as a first birthday gift for the Milne's only child, Christopher Robin. He quickly became Christopher Robin's constant companion but was initially known simply as Bear, Teddy or, more formally, Edward Bear. The rather peculiar name by which he was to become world famous was probably given to him in 1924 or 1925, an amalgamation of the name of an American black bear at London Zoo that the Milnes enjoyed watching (Winnie), and the nickname Christopher

Robin had used for a swan he used to see swimming on a lake in Arundel (Pooh). The two names were strung together, giving rise to Winnie-the-Pooh.

Milne, a successful playwright, was captivated by his young son and decided to immortalise his infancy in a collection of poems which were published by *Punch* magazine early in 1924 and later that year reproduced in a volume entitled *When We Were Very Young*. One of these poems, entitled 'Teddy Bear', tells the story of a rather fat teddy who eventually comes to terms with his size. The bear in the illustration opposite by E.H. Shepard is recognizable as the one Shepard drew in the Winnie-the-Pooh books, although he is not referred to by this name in the poem. Interestingly, Shepard's inspiration for Pooh came not from

LEFT: A.A. Milne, Winnie-the-Pooh and Christopher.
BELOW: Winnie and Friends (New York Public Library).

OPPOSITE: An E.H. Shepard illustration of Winnie-the-Pooh with Piglet.

Christopher Robin's teddy but from his own son Graham's bear called Growler. Graham Shepard was about 13 years older than Christopher Robin Milne, and Growler was therefore an earlier teddy – in appearance quite unlike the Farnell bear of 1921. Sadly, we are unable to compare the two side-by-side because Growler was destroyed by a dog in 1940. There is some speculation that he might have been a Steiff teddy but we shall probably never know for sure. The original Winnie-the-Pooh is still very much in existence; together with most of Christopher Robin's other famous toys he resides in a glass case in the New York Public Library. Milne himself decided the toys should go to the USA;

he allowed his American agent to take them on a tour of the United States and he felt they should stay on after they got a rapturous welcome. The warmth of the American response to Pooh and co. was in sharp contrast to Christopher Robin's indifference to his old toys, but then they had been something of a millstone around his neck since he was a very small boy. Although Shepard's illustrations are charming and evocative, it can be argued that they represent the Winnie-the-Pooh of fiction rather than reality. Likewise Disney's Pooh, both reviled and loved in almost equal measure, represents yet another version, no less true to the original than Shepard's.

A 10-in (25.5-cm) partially jointed Winnie-the-Pooh, created by Gabrielle Designs for his 70th anniversary, together with a smaller but fully jointed 4¹/₂-in (11.5-cm) Pooh by Hermann Teddy Original.

In October 1926, Milne followed the success of *When We Were Very Young* with the publication of *Winnie-the-Pooh*. Like its predecessor, it received rave reviews on both sides of the Atlantic, as did its follow-up, *The House at Pooh Corner* and a second volume of verses, *Now We Are Six*. While the gentle antics of Pooh and his Hundred Acre Wood chums had touched the hearts of millions, it's debatable whether the books were loved more by the children they were written for, than by the parents who bought them. One thing we know for certain, like teddy bears in general, today Winnie-the-Pooh has as many adult fans as juvenile ones.

EVERYONE KNOWS HIS NAME

While Winnie-the-Pooh entered the hall of fame in the 1920s because of a father immortalising his son's childhood, another iconic teddy burst onto the literary scene during the same decade in very different circumstances. Rupert Bear, created for the UK's *Daily Express* newspaper in 1920 by the artist Mary Tourtel, was introduced specifically to rival the *Daily Mail's* successful Teddy Tail character (a mouse, incidentally, rather than a bear as the name might suggest). The ploy worked, because Teddy Tail disappeared from print years ago but Rupert is still very much with us. In fact, he is the world's longest-running children's comic

A 14-in (35-cm) Rupert Bear, made by Real Soft Toys under licence to Express Newspapers.

MONSTER RUPERT

BY
MARY TOURTEL

character and he has an army of devoted fans of all ages. Today's Rupert looks very similar to Tourtel's original, although his check trousers are yellow rather than gray and his sweater has changed from blue to red. Rupert Annuals have been published since 1936 and are now sought-after collectors' items, and a fan club called 'The Followers of Rupert' was established in 1983 with the aim of bringing together adult enthusiasts. He has starred in his own TV show and been the subject of a hit song by Sir Paul McCartney, and his fame has spread far beyond the British Isles with the Dutch, in particular, taking this quintessentially English bear to their hearts.

RUDOLPH'S RIVAL

As with Rupert, commerce was behind the creation of a literary teddy bear called Punkinhead, a comical looking teddy with a tufty topknot who owes his existence in a round about way to Rudolph the Red-Nosed Reindeer. In December 1939, the American Montgomery Ward department store chain introduced Rudolph as a Christmas marketing device. He caught on in a big way, much to the envy of the store's competitors, and in 1948 one of these, the Canadian chain Eaton's, decided to fight back with their own Christmas creation. They came up with a storybook called *The Sad Little Bear*, in which the hero Punkinhead, doesn't

RIGHT: Merrythought's Punkinhead, minus his red trousers.

OPPOSITE: An early Rupert book showing Mary Tourtel's bear wearing a blue jumper and gray trousers.

fit in with his peers because of his odd topknot – much the same way that Rudolph's shiny red nose makes him a loner. All eventually comes right for Punkinhead when he gets to appear in Santa's Christmas parade. It's worth mentioning that the artist responsible for creating Punkinhead was Charlie Thorsen who also created a little known Disney character called Max Hare. Many animation experts believe that Max Hare was the very first incarnation of the carrot-munching rabbit known the world over as Bugs Bunny. Punkinhead was an enormous hit with the Canadian public. He appeared in further storybooks, led the store's annual Christmas parade and quickly became a merchandising gold mine, appearing on high chairs, watches, lamps, sheet music, rugs and so on. His fame outside his native country is largely due to Eaton's choice of the English Merrythought firm to produce their little hero as a plush toy. Renowned for their high quality products, Merrythought have an enthusiastic international following and early Punkinheads are one of their most sought-after products, fetching between $1,140–$1,530 when they come up for sale at auction.

MEANWHILE, FROM DARKEST PERU ...

While Punkinhead came from Canada, Darkest Peru was the origin of a much more famous literary teddy bear created by Michael Bond, a BBC TV cameraman who supplemented his income by writing radio plays and stories. On a rainy Christmas Eve, 1956, Bond missed his bus home and decided to while away the time before the next one by browsing in Selfridges department store. In the toy department he took pity on a small bear that had been left unwanted on a shelf. The asking price was seven shillings and sixpence, pretty much all the money Bond had with him. He bought the bear as an extra Christmas gift for his wife, Brenda, and it was given the name Paddington. The teddy prompted Bond to write a story about a bear called Paddington who arrives in London from Darkest Africa. When his agent read the story, he pointed out that there had been no bears in Africa for centuries and so Darkest Peru replaced Darkest Africa.

A Bear Called Paddington was published by Collins in 1958, with illustrations by the artist Peggy Fortnum. It became

ABOVE: Gabrielle Designs' Paddington.

OPPOSITE: Peggy Fortnum's illustration of Paddington Bear.

a bestseller within a year, and was swiftly translated into many other languages. *More About Paddington* was published in the UK in 1959, while *A Bear Called Paddington* was published to great acclaim in the US in 1960. Some reviewers liked it so much they predicted that it would stand next to Winnie-the-Pooh in popularity, and they have been proved right, as Paddington is probably the only bear that comes close to rivalling Milne's ursine superstar. Since then, over 150 Paddington books (including activity and board books for the very young) have been published, and in 1988 a sort of biography called *The Life and Times of Paddington Bear* was co-written by Russell Ash and Michael Bond.

The first soft toy version of Paddington was created by a Yorkshire-based company called Gabrielle Designs that was run by a skilled seamstress called Shirley Clarkson. Her children loved the Paddington books so for Christmas 1971, Shirley decided to make one for each of them. (Incidentally, one of those children is now the outspoken English motoring journalist and TV presenter Jeremy Clarkson and rumor has it that this bane of the environmentalist movement does not appreciate being reminded of his Paddington connection.) Gabrielle Designs secured a licence to manufacture Paddington Bears in 1972, and even though the firm ceased doing business in the mid-1990s, for many people their shaggy 19-in (48-cm) bears remain the definitive Paddington. Other firms have made very creditable versions, however, including Eden Toys, Rainbow Designs and Steiff, and although the Gabrielle Paddington is universally loved, the R. John Wright Dolls interpretation from 2000 is considered by many to resemble the original Peggy Fortnum illustrations more closely than any of the others.

BELOW: Gabrielle Designs' Aunt Lucy.

OPPOSITE: R. John Wright's Paddington from 2000.

The original Jane Hissey toys, including Old Bear
(top right) and Bramwell Brown (in red trousers).

One of the most recent heroes of teddy bear literature is Old Bear, created by art teacher-turned illustrator and writer Jane Hissey. Old Bear made his first appearance in a book of the same name published in 1986. The story concerned the attempts of his friends Bramwell Brown (a brown teddy bear), Little Bear, Duck and Rabbit to rescue the elderly teddy from the attic in which he had been placed for safe keeping. The combination of beautiful illustrations and a good story well told made Old Bear and his chums an immediate international success. The follow-up book, *Little Bear's Trousers*, was equally popular and from then on Hissey kept busy writing and illustrating new stories to keep up with demand, while raising her young family. While all the characters in the various books are funny and well-defined, it is Old Bear with his gentle wisdom who stands out, with his faithful friend Bramwell Brown running a close second.

The Old Bear stories have been animated for television and have been sold on video and audio tape. The main toys – Old Bear, Bramwell Brown, Little Bear, Rabbit, Duck and Ruff (a dog) – were produced in soft toy form by Golden Bear Toys in 1990 although they were not widely available and can be hard to find today. More recently, Royal Doulton produced a range of 20 Old Bear and Friends figurines, depicting the toys in various scenes from the books. Although the range has now been retired, the pieces are quite easy to find as collectables.

Countless other teddy bears have delighted us since the Roosevelt Bears made their mark with rhyming couplets in the early twentieth century. Most, like Teddy Robinson, Teddy Edward, The Berensteins and The Upstairs Downstairs Bears were written for children but a few, notably Aloysius from Evelyn Waugh's *Brideshead Revisited* and John Betjeman's Archibald Ormsby Gore, make their appearances in adult-oriented literature. The truth is that teddy bears have found a comfortable niche in the publishing world and they show no sign of vacating it. At this very moment somewhere on earth, an author is probably working on the next big teddy bear book, secure in the knowledge that there will always be a warm reception for a teddy hero.

Old Bear, produced by Golden Bear Toys in 1990.

Think of a teddy bear, and rich, vibrant colors do not automatically spring to mind. For most people, 'proper' teddy bears come in every shade of brown, gold, honey and beige, while bears in black or white are less common but still acceptable. Yet there is a tradition of brightly colored teds that stretches back to the earliest years of the teddy bear's life and continues to this day. We know that Steiff experimented with color as early as 1908, offering sample bears in bright green, yellow, pink and blue mohair to English toy buyers that year. They were bright, fun and colorful, but the public was not yet ready for bears in such unnatural colors, so they were never marketed. The samples

themselves went missing, although the blue one reappeared in 1993 when he became the star of Christie's first-ever dedicated teddy bear auction. By this time he had a name – Elliot – and his reception was far warmer than it had been in 1908, with enthusiasts falling over themselves to own him. After a barrage of bidding, he sold for $94,420 to a Canadian collector.

Just four or five years after their bright bears were rejected by the English market, Steiff launched another colorful teddy much more successfully into the US. Dolly Bär, with a red mohair body, white mohair head and blue neck ruff, was created in 1913 to celebrate the

LEFT: Elliot, the 1908 blue Steiff sample bear sold at Christie's in 1993.
BELOW: A modern Steiff replica of the 1908 green bear that never made it onto the market.

OPPOSITE: Steiff's Dolly Bär, dating from 1913, was created specifically for the American market; the blue ruff has faded over time.

inauguration of Woodrow Wilson who had won the presidential election held in November 1912. From now on, patriotism had a significant role to play in the development of the colorful teddy. In America, for example, teddy bears combining the red, white and blue of 'Old Glory' found a ready market and during the First World War, the British firm Farnell created tiny good-luck bears in red, white and blue mohair for soldiers heading for the Front. Just under 40 years later, Merrythought was inspired to create a red, white and blue mohair plush teddy to commemorate Queen Elizabeth II's coronation.

TOP: Lavender, a purple mohair teddy bear of German origin, dating from the 1930s.
ABOVE (left): A bright red, open-mouthed teddy, maker unknown, with velvet paw pads and mouth.
(right): A pink mohair teddy, circa 1925.

OPPOSITE: This Farnell teddy bear dating from the late 1920s is made from beautiful turquoise mohair.

THE JAZZ AGE

It took more than national pride to make the colorful teddy really catch on, however. In fact, it was largely a reaction to the misery caused by the First World War that laid the groundwork for their popularity. After the end of the conflict, people wanted to forget its horrors and a hedonistic, live-for-the-moment attitude was common among many. Novelty and excitement were the order of the day and, teddy bears in safe, traditional colors were considered a little tame, so many manufacturers introduced bears in vivid hues to liven up their catalogs. This was an era that embraced the acid palette of Clarice Cliff's ceramics so it's not surprising that jazzy teds should also have found a welcome. In the period between the wars, leading firms including Farnell, Chad Valley, Merrythought and Hermann created bears in almost every shade known to nature. Red, turquoise, blue, green, purple and pink were just some of the vibrant colors that kept the teddy in demand. As previously seen on pages 55 and 56, the German company Schuco went one better, producing brightly colored miniature bears that doubled as scent bottles, compacts and lipstick holders. For a time, a colorful teddy was the ultimate accessory for any fashionable Jazz Age flapper.

The Second World War saw a dramatic reduction in teddy bear production and any teddy bears that were made had to be created from whatever material was available. Mohair was needed to make warm hats and gloves for the war effort so manufacturers started making a different sort of colorful teddy with only its head and paws made of mohair and the rest of the body 'dressed' in cotton or felt. After the war, brightly colored bears continued to be made but never in the numbers that their popular brown and gold cousins were produced. Pink and blue bears became popular gifts for newborn babies, but brown, beige, gold and honey were always the most common teddy tints.

THE ARTISAN EIGHTIES

This love for the traditional muted tones might have continued forever had it not been for the advent of the teddy bear artists in the 1980s. Many of these home-based craftspeople designed their own teddy patterns and made them as one-off pieces or in small limited

ABOVE: Some contemporary bears make subtle use of color, as with the Cotswold Bear Company's lilac-tipped Mischief and Melody.

LEFT: A traditional-style teddy created by US artist Kathleen Wallace in sparse, bright blue mohair.

OPPOSITE (top): Oo'er by Barbara-Ann Bears; zingy colors in unusual combinations create a teddy that is utterly untraditional and yet massively appealing.

(left): Rainbow Dreamer, a unique teddy bear made from mohair that was hand dyed by UK artist Rita Harwood.

(right): Tequila Sunrise created by Austrian teddy bear artist Renate Hanisch who painstakingly hand-dyed the mohair to achieve the graduated effect.

edition sets. In the early days of teddy bear artistry, designs were fairly conventional – partly because that was what the market wanted and partly because the only materials available were very traditional. As popularity for the artisan bears grew, however, the amount of mohair and other essential bear-making materials increased and greater choice gradually became available. The creative wheel started turning with more choice leading to increased creativity, and by the 1990s highly original and innovative teddy bears were being made, many of them in exuberant, jewel-like shades that would have found favor with the novelty-seeking folk of the 1920s.

Today there are a number of extremely successful artists who specialize in bears made of various shades of mohair, sometimes in deliberately clashing colors. To the untrained eye the effect looks startling, but teddy aficionados understand that it takes great skill and precision to dye the mohair and create the overall effect. Other artists prefer to use gentler colors, sometimes to recreate traditional-style teddy bears and sometimes to take the basic teddy design and alter

and exaggerate certain features, ending up with something unique and wonderful. After a long and troubled childhood, the bright and beautiful teddy bear has finally come of age.

Having spent most of the last 90 years with no clothes on, latter-day teddy bears have taken to dressing up with glorious enthusiasm. The increase in contemporary look-alike teddy bears was discussed in Chapter Two, but the 'Who Am I?' trend doesn't end there. With public interest in history at an all-time high, some teddy makers find the lure of the dressing-up-box impossible to resist. With thousands of historical figures, and the entire back catalog of characters from classic literature for inspiration, it looks as if the phenomenon of the costume drama teddy will be around for a while to come.

THE EVACUEE

One of the first bear makers to venture into the realms of historically inspired teddy bears was English artist Jo Greeno. Jo switched to bear making after a highly successful career in teaching, becoming head teacher of a primary school. Although there is no immediate link between the two occupations, Jo has used her teaching skills to impart her bear-making knowledge to a new generation of would-be teddy artists. Also, the high degree of professionalism Jo acquired while teaching has helped her establish a worldwide reputation for excellence in the teddy bear market, to the extent that she featured on the front page of the *Wall Street Journal* back in 1993. Over the years Jo has made some memorable bears, but the piece for which she is best known is The Evacuee, which was inspired by photographs of teddy-clutching children being evacuated from London during the Second World War. Sent to the relative safety of the countryside to live with strangers, these children had no idea when they would next see their parents, so for many of them, their teddy bears were a vital comfort. Jo's Evacuee bears wear beautifully tailored clothing appropriate to the

era, and they all carry their own bears or soft toys. As the final touch of poignant realism, each bear has a luggage label inscribed with the evacuee's intended destination.

TEDDY GET YOUR GUN!

Another designer who has enthusiastically helped the 'teddy from history's' popularity is New Zealand's Robin Rive. Although Robin creates many bears without a historical reference, she'll seize on a particular anniversary or centenary to produce a themed limited edition teddy. Her 2006 interpretations of Annie Oakley and Wild Bill Hickok stand out in particular as they feature bears with hair – moustache and beard in the case of Wild Bill and neatly tied braids in the case of gun-toting Annie. Robin has also looked to great literature for artistic inspiration. We have seen Shakespeare's doomed lovers Romeo and Juliet, for example, and Hamlet and Ophelia have also taken the teddy stage. Perhaps her most elegant literary creations, however, are Miss Elizabeth Bennet and Mr Darcy, inspired by the main characters from Jane Austen's masterpiece, *Pride and Prejudice*.

Adored as *Pride and Prejudice* is by the public and television and film producers, it is small wonder that its

CLOCKWISE (from top left): Robin Rive's limited edition Annie Oakley; Wild Bill, an limited edition interpretation of Wild Bill Hickok by Robin Rive; Everyone's favorite lovers from literature, Miss Elizabeth Bennett and Mr Darcy, created as a limited edition by Robin Rive.

OPPOSITE: The Evacuees by Jo Greeno.

main characters have found their way into the teddy bear world. What is surprising, however, is that Jonathan Swift's epic, *Gulliver's Travels*, should have received similar treatment. After all, this is a lengthy and complex work of literature that is not as easily read and enjoyed as a Jane Austen novel. Despite this, Canadian bear maker Trish Pilon was inspired by the book to create a teddy version of Gulliver in Lilliput. It's a clever piece that shows great skill from the artist, both for creating the bears and for dressing Gulliver in a costume that's authentically 17th century.

THE TOAST OF SALZBURG

Literature is not the only art form to lend its superstars to the teddy bear world – music and fine art have also done their bit. In 2006, celebrations to mark the bicentenary of the birth of Mozart inspired the German company Teddy Hermann to create a splendid limited edition Mozart bear. Wearing a meticulous wig, made from mink plush, the bear is dressed in a velvet frock coat and georgette jabot.

ABOVE: Gulliver and the Lilliputians by Trish Pilon.
RIGHT: Mozart, a limited edition from Teddy Hermann.

STATESMEN AND SOLDIERS

Politicians often have colorful private lives but they are rarely regarded as heroic figures, at least in their own lifetimes. For that reason, we are unlikely to see Tony Blair or George W. Bush bears on the market any time soon (although there has already been an Angela Merkel bear), but political figures from history are a different matter. In recent times Robin Rive has produced successful teddy versions of Abraham Lincoln, Thomas Jefferson and Winston Churchill, while Australian artist Lisa Rosenbaum has also tackled Abe Lincoln as a subject, creating a highly original bear that features a portrait of the great man in oils on the bear's body. The single item of clothing used on this

Furthermore, since Mozart without music is unthinkable, the teddy carries a violin and is fitted with a music box that plays *Eine Kleine Nachtmusik*. Another Teddy Hermann creation in 2006 celebrated the 400th anniversary of the birth of Rembrandt. This time the costume was less elaborate, relying on a fur-trimmed coat and a black velvet painter's cap to suggest the identity of the bear, although a paintbrush fixed to its left paw gave a strong hint! Still on the subject of art, artist Maria Collin created a brilliant teddy bear vignette, paying tribute to a famous painting rather than its painter. With great wit and flair, Maria reinterpreted Manet's famous painting *Déjeuner sur l'herbe* to feature teddy bears instead of people. The two male bears are dressed in the appropriate costume of the era, while the voluptuous lady bear is left unclothed.

ABOVE: A limited edition Rembrandt by Teddy Hermann.
RIGHT: Teddy Bears' Picnic (after Manet), created by Maria Collin.

is a good example of this genre; the exquisitely crafted, traditional-style teddy sits in a suitably battered old suitcase, surrounded by vintage accessories.

Popular as they are with many people, dressed teddy bears are not to everyone's taste. Some find them a little cutesy, while others think that teddy bears made from beautiful mohair need no other adornment. There's probably something to be said for both arguments, but even so, when they are done well, costumed teddy bears have an allure that's hard to resist.

bear is a top hat, but a clever use of color and portraiture creates the overall effect of a costumed teddy.

Military figures are also popular subjects for bear makers, probably because a uniformed teddy cuts a dashing figure. This became apparent as early as 1916 when an English firm called Harwin produced a range known as the Ally Bears, featuring teddy bears dressed in the uniforms of the British armed forces and their allies. Patriotic fervor made these teds very popular, and it was not uncommon for a child to own a teddy dressed in the uniform of his or her father's regiment. They went out of favor when the war ended but are now back in vogue, appreciated by today's collectors for their evocative appeal.

Another style that suits the teddy bear is that of the aviation hero. A number of international bear makers have created 'flying ace' bears and they have proved to be very popular, with men frequently falling for their *Boys' Own* charms. Dutch artist Marjoleine Diemel's Flying Dutchman

ABOVE: A vintage Ally Bear by Harwin.
LEFT: Abe Lincoln, a stunning creation from Lisa Rosenbaum.

OPPOSITE: Marjoleine Diemel's Flying Dutchman.

9 MODERN MASTERPIECES

Today, more than 100 years after its invention, the teddy bear continues to be a highly popular toy. A teddy is an obvious choice of gift for a newborn baby and, as the baby progresses through childhood, he or she is likely to acquire at least a few more. (Most children will happily admit to owning 'hundreds' of teddy bears, but if you look closer, many of these toys will be cuddly dogs, lambs and so on. This trend for children to refer to any old stuffed toy as a teddy is still fairly recent, but hopefully parents will help maintain the distinction, since asking a teddy to assume the identity of any stuffed toy animal is stretching its ability as a master of disguise a little too far.) Without a doubt, children's teddy bears today are loved by their young owners, but it's unlikely they will become desirable collectors' items in the future. This is partly because of the vast numbers produced and partly because they are not particularly exciting in design terms. The burden for ensuring that future generations will hold 21st century teddy bears in high regard falls to the creators of teddy bears specifically targeted at the adult market. When it comes to contemporary collectable teddy bears, there are two specific genres available – the manufactured and the artist-made. Both types have made occasional appearances elsewhere in the book, but the focus of this chapter is firmly on the artist-made variety, because the level of skill, ingenuity and sheer effort involved in making these creations deserves greater awareness.

BORN IN THE USA

The teddy bear artist first appeared in the USA in the 1970s, when an awakened interest in vintage bears as collectable items motivated doll makers and crafters to try their hand at creating individual teddy bears. By the 1980s the trend had spread to Europe, Canada, Australia and New Zealand, and the 1990s saw bear artistry established in South Africa and much of the Far East. Initially, artist bears were fairly traditional in appearance, partly because the public was not ready for anything more innovative, but mainly because the limited choice of bear-making materials only lent themselves to traditional styles. As more people turned to bear artistry, however, other materials were used, and increasingly inventive teddy bears started to appear. Today, the incredible diversity of styles is one of the main attractions for those who collect artist-made bears. There's no end to the different ways bear artists reinterpret the basic teddy design, and the best artists are continually stretching themselves to develop new techniques or styles.

CREATING A MASTERPIECE

So what is the definition of a bear artist? The simplest explanation of the term is someone who designs their teddy bears from scratch, creating their own patterns and using their own skills to make the finished article. To do this well can be difficult enough, but the most inspiring artists are those who experiment until they produce something fresh, with perhaps a particular feature or technique that has not been seen before. The difference between a good bear artist and a great one is similar to the distinction between a painter who produces attractive, conventional works and one who uses vision to create something exceptional – maybe using unexpected methods to achieve a desired outcome. Some collectors put great store in a bear being hand stitched but

OPPOSITE: Tiger Feet, an irresistible open-mouthed teddy created by Paula Carter (All Bear).

LEFT: Buster, by Art Rogers (Chatham Village Bears); Art has a Master of Fine Arts degree from Washington University.

OPPOSITE: Alvin was made by popular South African artist Janet Changfoot (Changle Bears).

this is not necessarily an advantage. For a start, the seams of machine-stitched teddy bears may be more durable than hand sewn ones, and in any case it takes skill to achieve a good result whichever method is used. As with any type of art, personal taste determines whether or not someone likes a piece, but even so, with the very best artist-made teddy bears it is possible to admire the creative talent that went into making them without necessarily liking the end result.

Today, bear artistry as a career is flourishing globally, thanks to the opportunities it gives individuals to find fulfilling employment at home (the overwhelming majority of bear artists are home workers). Most of these artists are women but a significant number of men have made their mark, including Gregory Gyllenship from the UK, Audie Sison from Holland and Art Rogers from the USA. Art, who sells his bears under the Chatham Village Bears label, has developed a highly distinctive style, popular with

collectors at home and abroad. In selling to an international market Art is not alone, since most accomplished bear artists find customers worldwide, and they have been able to do this largely due to the Internet. Almost all professional bear artists have their own websites, and a number of them use Internet auction sites to market their work further. As well as having a website, the bear artist must be willing to travel to different countries if he or she wants to encourage an international following. Major teddy bears shows are held regularly in the USA, Japan, Korea, Taiwan, and throughout Europe, and those artists who are prepared to pack up their teddy bears and travel to these events are generally well rewarded by the sales they generate. South African artist Janet Changfoot exhibits at events in the UK twice a year, and her stand frequently empties of bears within an hour of the show opening. That said, if travel is out of the question for any reason, a good

ABOVE (top): Gifts Within is a 29-in (74-cm) painted bear made by the talented Lisa Rosenbaum (Oz Matilda Bear Co). (above): Eva and Günter Dufeu (Dufeu Bears) specialise in old-style teddy bears.

OPPOSITE: Salo, a 16-in (40-cm) clown panda teddy, was a new departure for Dutch artist Ellen Borggreve.

website can certainly go a long way to compensate. Successful UK artist Paula Carter rarely exhibits outside the UK but she has a healthy international following, nurtured by her excellent website that has the facility to translate pages into a number of foreign languages. Exquisitely crafted teddy bears and a professional, welcoming website are enough to maintain Paula's position as a leading global artist, with collectors as far afield as Australia, the Far East, America and South Africa.

Thanks to the Internet and all the international travel, a sort of global teddy bear community has developed, in which artists and collectors get to know one another. Friendships are born, advice is shared and rising talent is swiftly recognised and encouraged. Among the other important features of the bear community are the specialist teddy magazines that promote bear artistry and keep collectors up-to-date with news about all aspects of their hobby. Most countries in which bear artists operate have at least one of these magazines, and it's common for enthusiasts to subscribe to international titles to keep abreast of developments overseas. For bear lovers at least, the world really is shrinking, and the teddy bear has found yet another new role – this time as an ambassador of international goodwill.

TEDDY ART: A NEW GENRE

There are so many excellent bear artists operating worldwide that it would be impossible to mention them all in this chapter. Those featured here represent just the tip of the iceberg, and have been chosen both for the quality of their work and because few, if any, have featured in previous books. With such a wealth of talent in the world of teddy bear artistry, it really is time artist-made bears were granted a wider appreciation as works of art. The trouble is that once most people hear the words 'teddy bear', they immediately think of something cute, cuddly and familiar, finding it hard to adjust to the idea of teddies as works of art. Yet anyone studying bears made by the UK's Jean and Bill Ashburner, Australia's Lisa Rosenbaum, Holland's Ellen Borggreve, Germany's Dufeu Bears, Belgium's Helga Torfs or the USA's Michelle Lamb, for example, should at once be able to recognise the artistic merit in their work.

Another obstacle to overcome before artist-made teddy bears gain the widespread recognition they deserve is the indignant response of 'I'm not paying that for a teddy bear!' made by many people on seeing an artist bear's price tag. At first glance, it may seem that prices for the crème-de-la-crème of artist-made bears are high, but creating any work of art is always labor-intensive and many hours are spent crafting these bears. Add to that the high cost of the materials – mohair alone is very expensive – and the additional cost of exhibiting at shows and running a website, and it quickly becomes apparent that the price tags are more than justified. There should be no reason why an artist-made teddy should not carry the same cachet as, say, a piece of first-rate studio pottery or modern sculpture. Here's hoping that such appreciation is just around the corner.

CLOCKWISE (from below): Skill and artistic vision are needed to make an original bear like Angel (Melanie Jayne Bears); making fine miniature teddy bears is an art in itself, one that Miriam Baker, creator of this exquisite, fully jointed 4-in (10-cm) bear, has mastered to perfection; Belgium's Helga Torfs has a worldwide reputation for her characterful teddy bears, typified by Choky Drops.

OPPOSITE: Multi-award-winning Michelle Lamb (One&Only Bears) created Maverick, a teddy rich in artistic detail.

ESSENTIAL TEDDY DIRECTORY

If, as I hope, reading this book has fired your enthusiasm for teddy bears, you may be keen to find out more about them. To gain knowledge and experience, nothing beats looking at and, where possible, touching bears – museums are good for the former and auctions for the latter. Talking to specialist dealers can also be useful as they are often happy to share their expertise. If, on the other hand, you feel ready to begin a collection, you'll probably want to start visiting fairs and shops, and browsing artist websites. In either case, to get you started I have listed a few suggestions that should prove useful. This is by no means a definitive list – there are literally thousands of teddy bear shops, museums, fairs and so on for you to discover – but these are a few of my personal favorites.

MUSEUMS

The Puppenhausmuseum
Basel
Switzerland
www.puppenhausmuseum.ch

The Puppenhausmuseum has an extensive and impressive collection of vintage teddy bears from all the major manufacturers, including many rare and important pieces. The teddy bears are displayed in purpose-built wood and glass cabinets, and are arranged in delightful scenes which utilize other vintage toys and objects. It is a joy to visit.

The World of Steiff
Giengen/Brenz
Germany
www.steiff.com

The World of Steiff is a state of the art museum-cum-experience which was opened in the teddy bear's birthplace, Giengen, Germany, in 2005. An imaginative tour takes the visitor through the history of the teddy bear and culminates in the Steiff museum where many teddy treasures are on display. A wonderful experience for all the family.

V&A Museum of Childhood
London
England
http://www.vam.ac.uk/moc/

Part of London's famous Victoria & Albert Museum but housed separately in Bethnal Green, the museum offers, amongst other things, an interesting collection of vintage teddy bears.

(Try also The Izu Teddy Bear Museum, Japan – www.teddynet. co.jp/izu/izu – and The Jeju Teddy Bear Museum, Korea – www.teddybearmuseum.com/eng)

SPECIALIST TEDDY BEAR SHOPS

The Toy Shoppe
11632 Busy Street
Richmond
VA 23236
www.thetoyshoppe.com

Bear Paths
2815 Jay Avenue
Cleveland
OH 44113
www.bearpaths.com

Dollsville Dolls & Bearsville Bears
292 N. Palm Canyon, Palm Springs
CA 92262
www.dollsville.com.

(Try also The Bear Garden, Guildford, England – www.beargarden.co.uk; Meem's Dolls and Bears, Perth, Australia – www.meems-bears-dolls.com and L'Ours Du Marais, Paris, France – www.oursdumarais.com)

FAIRS

Teddy Bear Artist Invitational (TBAI)
4131 Rte 9,
Plattsburgh
NY 12901
email: info@tbai.org

This annual weekend event for teddy bear artists and collectors raises money for Ross Park Zoo with a series of activities including an auction and a fair.

The **London Teddy Bear Fair** takes place annually at the end of October in the beautiful surroundings of Alexandra Palace in North London, England. Organised by the UK's leading teddy bear magazine, *Teddy Bear Scene*, the event attracts exhibitors of the highest standard and is very popular with collectors.
www.warnersgroup.co.uk

The annual **Steiff Festival** is held in Giengen, Germany every summer. Dealers who specialise in Steiff items old and new converge on the pretty town for a Steiff-only fair.
www.steiff.com

(Try also Teddybär Total, Munster, Germany – www.teddybaertotal.de; Taiwan Teddy Bear Show, Taipei, Taiwan, – www.twtba.org.tw/english; Salon Gueules de Miel, Paris, France – www.salonagdm.com; International Doll and Teddy Bear Fair, Rotterdam, Holland – www.niesjewolters.nl and Japan Teddy Bear Convention, Tokyo, Japan – www.jteddy.net)

AUCTIONEERS

Christie's South Kensington
London
England
www.christies.co.uk

The twice yearly specialist teddy bear auctions held at Christie's offer collectors a good selection of vintage teddy bears within a varied price range. At the high end, very rare or special bears can sell for thousands of pounds but the majority are much more affordable. Sale viewings present a great opportunity to see and touch old bears, and the auctions themselves are lots of fun.

Vectis Auctions Ltd
Stockton-on-Tees
England
www.vectis.co.uk

Vectis hold regular specialist bear auctions, selling all types of teddy bears and soft toys including vintage, modern limited editions and artist-made bears.

Bonhams
London
England
www.bonhams.com/toys

Bonhams hold regular toy sales that include vintage teddy bears at their Knightsbridge saleroom and the one in Knowle in the Midlands.

DEALERS IN VINTAGE TEDDY BEARS

Sue Pearson Dolls & Teddy Bears
www.suepearson.co.uk

Bourton Bears
www.bourtonbears.com
A very extensive range of old teds to suit all pockets.

Bourton Bears exhibit at major bear fairs and also sell via their excellent website.

(Try also The Old Bear Company – www.oldbearcompany. com; The Teddy Bear Chest – www.theteddybearchest.co.uk and All You Can Bear – www.allyoucanbear.com.)

RESTORATION

Dot Bird
email: dotsbears@btinternet.com

Dot is a specialist in the sympathetic restoration of vintage teddy bears. She writes on the subject for *Teddy Bear Scene* magazine.

TEDDY BEAR ARTISTS

All Bear By Paula Carter
www.allbear.co.uk

Barbara-Ann Bears
www.barbara-annbears.com

Bears @ No. 27 (Renate Hanisch)
www.no27.at

Bear Bits
www.bearbits.com

Bear Treasures (Melanie Jayne)
www.beartreasures.com

Changle Bears (Janet Changfoot)
www.changlebears.homestead.com

Chatham Village Bears (Art Rogers)
www.chathamvillagebears.com

Dufeu-Bear (Eva and Gunther Dufeu)
www.dufeu-bear.de

Ellen Borggreve
www.ellen-borggreve.com

Helga Torfs
www.helgatorfs.com

Jo Greeno
 email jo.greeno@freezone.co.uk

Old Time Teddies (Marjoleine Diemel)
www.marjoleinediemel.nl

One & Only Bears (Michelle Lamb)
www.oneandonlybears.com

Oz Matilda Bears (Lisa Rosenbaum)
www.ozmatilda.com.au

Puca Bears (Maria Collin)
www.puca-bears.de

The Squire's Bears (Trish Pilon)
www.squire.hypermart.net

Woodland Teddies (Rita Harwood)
www.woodlandteddies.com

PUBLICATIONS

Teddy Bear & Friends
www.teddybearandfriends.com

Teddy Bear Review
www.teddybearreview.com.

Teddy Bear Scene & Other Furry Friends
www.teddybearscene.co.uk

The UK's leading teddy bear publication, which also has a wide international readership. Published monthly, it covers all aspects of teddy bear collecting.

The UK Teddy Bear Guide
www.hugglets.co.uk

Published by Hugglets, this is an invaluable reference source for teddy bear shops, fairs, artists etc. Also covers international subjects.

Christie's Century of Teddy Bears

By Leyla Maniera. This excellent book looks at the history of the teddy bear in detail.

ACKNOWLEDGEMENTS

A great many people gave me invaluable assistance whilst I was writing this book and I want them to know how deeply I appreciate their help. Firstly, I must thank Leyla Maniera whose passion for teddy bears is equalled only by her knowledge of them. Much gratitude is due also to Merrythought's Peter Andrews who was always willing to rummage through the archives in search of an elusive picture, and who gave me lots of encouragement as I was working on this project.

Others to whom I am indebted include Margarete Steiff GmbH, Hermann Teddy Original, Ian Pout, proprietor of Teddy Bears of Witney, Laura Sinanovitch of the marvellous Puppenhausmuseum, Daniel Agnew, teddy bear specialist at Christie's South Kensington, Vectis Auctions, Sue and Jasper Pearson from Sue Pearson Dolls & Teddy Bears, Pat Rush, Robin Rive, The Cotswold Bear Co, Boyds Bears, Dot Bird, Paula Carter, Vicky Gwilliam, Mel and Andy from Bourton Bears, Natalie Hartman Whitnack and The Bear Museum, Petersfield. Also to be thanked are the many talented artists, too numerous to mention individually, who generously allowed me to feature their work in this book, and my friend and fellow teddy enthusiast Tamsie Duffin, who read the manuscript and gave me lots of encouragement.

To my husband, Alastair, I give grateful thanks for his love, patience and support, and the same goes to my daughter Amy for her enormous enthusiasm for this project. Finally, I must acknowledge my many wonderful, amazingly varied teddy bears because their rich diversity provided the inspiration for this book.

PICTURE CREDITS

The publishers would like to thank the following for providing images and for permission to reproduce copyright material. While every effort has been made to trace and acknowledge all copyright holders, we would like to apologize should there have been any errors or omissions.

p4 Christie's (far left), Steiff (far right); p5 Steiff; p6 Steiff; p7 Seiff (top left); p9 Sue Pearson (top right), Puppenhausmuseum (bottom left); p10 Puppenhausmuseum; p11 Bear Museum, Petersfield; p12 Paula Carter (left), Vectis Auctions (top and bottom right); p13 Bourton Bears; p15 Merrythought; p17 Merrythought; p20 Sue Pearson; p21 Sue Pearson (top left), Steiff (top right), Merrythought (bottom left); p23 Robin Rive (top), Merrythought (bottom); p25 Robin Rive bottom right); p26 Hermann Teddy original (left), Boyds (right); p27 Helga Torfs; p28 Robin Rive (right); p29 Pat Rush; p37 Ian Pout, Teddy Bears of Witney; p38 Christie's; p39 Ian Pout, Teddy Bears of Witney; p40 Ian Pout, Teddy Bears of Witney; p41 Christie's; p42 Steiff; p43 Steiff; pp44 & 45 Steiff; p46 Lisa Rosenbaum; p47 Michelle Lamb; p49 Christie's; p50 Steiff; p51 Ian Pout, Teddy Bears of Witney; p53 Dot Bird (far right, top and bottom), Merrythought (left); p55 Dot Bird (top), Puppenhausmuseum (bottom); p56 Puppenhausmuseum; p57 Backpack Toys; p59 Hermann Teddy Original; p60 © National Portrait Gallery, London (top), The New York Public Library (bottom); p61 © The Estate of E.H. Shepard; p64 Rupert®, © Entertainment Rights Distribution Limited/Express Newspapers 2007; p65 Merrythought; p67 PADDINGTON BEAR™ © Paddington and Company Ltd 2006 Licensed by ©opyrights Group Paddington Bear™, Paddington™ and PB™ are trademarks of Paddington and Company Ltd; p70 Jane Hissey; p72 Puppenhausmuseum; p73 Christie's (left); Steiff (right); p74 Sue Pearson (bottom 2); p75 Christie's; p76 Cotswold Bear Company (top); p77 Barbara-Ann Bears (top right), Rita Harwood (bottom left), Renate Hanisch (bottom right); p78 Jo Greeno; p79 Robin Rive (both images); p80 Trish Pilon (top); Hermann Teddy Original (bottom); p81 Hermann Teddy Original (top); Maria Collin (bottom); p82 Lisa Rosenbaum (left), Pat Rush (right); p83 Marjoleine Diemel; p86 Janet Changfoot; p87 Art Rogers; p88 Lisa Rosenbaum (top), Dufeu Bears (bottom); p89 Ellen Borggreve; p90 Michelle Lamb; p91 Helga Torfs (left), Bear Treasures (top right).